# THE
# PROMISE
## TO THE ONE

# THE
# PROMISE
## TO THE ONE

## JASON HEWLETT

# DEDICATION

———

*I dedicate this book to you, the Reader.*

*You are The One...*

*the Legendary Leader whose Signature Moves will change the world.*

*Rediscover The Promise in yourself,*

*and live out your Calling as only you can.*

Published and distributed by:
SOUND WISDOM
P.O. Box 310
Shippensburg, PA 17257-0310
717-530-2122

info@soundwisdom.com

www.soundwisdom.com

While efforts have been made to verify information contained in this publication, neither the author nor the publisher assumes any responsibility for errors, inaccuracies, or omissions. While this publication is chock-full of useful, practical information; it is not intended to be legal or accounting advice. All readers are advised to seek competent lawyers and accountants to follow laws and regulations that may apply to specific situations. The reader of this publication assumes responsibility for the use of the information. The author and publisher assume no responsibility or liability whatsoever on the behalf of the reader of this publication.

Cover design by Eileen Rockwell

ISBN 13 TP: 978-1-64095-193-8

ISBN 13 eBook: 978-1-64095-194-5

For Worldwide Distribution, Printed in the U.S.A.

3 4 5 6 7 8 / 24 23 22 21

# CONTENTS

# PREFACE

*The woods are lovely, dark and deep.*
*But I have promises to keep,*
*And miles to go before I sleep.*

—ROBERT FROST

Think back to when you were a child.

Did you have dreams that you would do great things? That you were meant for something magnificent? That you would leave a legacy that would be remembered by future generations?

These dreams never go away. They're always present, hidden under the noise of the everyday. Sometimes we are gripped with sudden anxiety, a memory of our childhood ambitions that quickly turns to guilt. This shift results from a fear that we will wake up—or already have woken up—to realize that we are living a life we weren't made to. Maybe *fear* and *guilt* aren't strong enough words—possibly *lifelong regret and dissatisfaction* are more like it. Facing this reality is like staring at your evil twin and evaluating all their missteps and shortcomings in life in relation to what they could have become, only to realize that you are in fact the twin who didn't stack up.

At some moment in your life, you made a subconscious Promise to yourself as to whether you would lean into your gifts and develop them and do whatever it took to keep this Promise—or whether you would allow life to gobble your ambitions, aspirations, and greatest dreams and stick you in the mediocrity line.

And yet here you are...only scratching the surface of your potential, your greatest purposes still unfulfilled.

So often we are upset about how the world seems to have broken its Promise to us, as if life is just so tough and unfair and filled with unreliable people who are constantly letting us down. The truth of the matter is, our failed commitments are the problem: when we break The Promise to ourselves, we have broken our Promise to The World.

*The Promise to The One* is a reminder of your original Promise to yourself about what you would make of your life.

It is also a call to action—a call to become a Legendary Leader by developing an unshakeable dedication to magnifying your Signature Moves, the unique talents you've been given to better your life as well as the lives of your family, community, and even the world.

You will receive within the following pages a formula for assessing your past actions, altering your current path, and keeping The Promise you once made.

This drive toward self-knowledge and purposeful action is the IDENTIFY • CLARIFY • MAGNIFY process that you'll learn in Chapter 2 of this book—a series of simple steps that will completely change the way you live every day from now on.

You will go from someone who ends the day wondering what you did and questioning whether it was of any worth in terms of your work and fulfillment to the type of person who can be counted on for anything and who receives opportunities, has happiness, and lives a life of complete joy and gratitude.

You will be the one who is trusted by your peers to give counsel, mentor, and serve on the highest level.

You will be the kind of spouse who is cherished and cared for and spoken of lovingly and admiringly, even by your spouse's friends.

You will be the kind of Mom or Dad that every kid would want to have.

You will have a career that makes a difference in the world, that serves exponentially, that provides in your stewardship, and that gives you life's great reward of *work well done*. Every single day.

You will grow your faith and relationship with God and the universe.

You will be able to look in the mirror and love what you see—a fine wine in the aging process, self-loving and self-forgiving.

You will learn to master your processes, systems, behaviors, and habits.

How can all of this be promised to you in one simple book? Well, it's not a Promise I make here; it's just a matter of fact: if you will put into application what you read moving forward, then you will make these changes—really, mental shifts—yourself. It's not a Promise from me; it's your Promise rediscovered in yourself.

Leading you on this journey is my life's Purpose, one that I've been pursuing ever since I was a child. Even when I went to bed as a kid, I remember lying there, looking at the ceiling, saying to myself, "I Promise to find a way to help others find their greatness."

There is a Legend in every person. You have Signature Moves that will change the world if you're willing to Magnify them. You have a Promise to share them with the world.

This is The Promise to The One.

## THE PROMISE JOURNAL

If you're like me, you've found that you have broken many Promises to yourself. This book is your wake-up call to the importance of those commitments. Your happiness, your relationships, your career, and your legacy all are at stake: Will you cultivate and share the gifts that you've been given so that you can live out your greatest Promise to Self—to live out your Calling?

Oftentimes the reason we fail to keep these Promises is because we simply forget that we made them in the first place. As Friedrich Nietzsche wrote, "One must have a good memory to be able to keep the promises one has given."[1] That is why it is crucial for you to buy and begin using a Promise Journal, in which you will record and track your Promise progress. A Promise Journal will enable you to become one of the rare individuals and leaders on the planet who diligently and actively keeps the Promises you've made to the world.

Whether you use a physical book or a digital journal, you will want to commit to writing in it regularly—to start, once per week, and more as the practice becomes integral to your routines and well-being. Have this journal by your side as you read this book, which will guide you through the process of IDENTIFYING, CLARIFYING, and MAGNIFYING your talents and so living out your Promises daily. Beyond being a practical method of mapping your journey, your Promise Journal will provide the necessary mindset to live The Promise at the level you are committing to do so.

## To begin this process:

Visit jasonhewlett.com/ThePromiseJournalGuide to access your free Promise Journal Guide, including a Promise Process Evaluation resource to help you determine your core Promises that the Journal will help you live out.

Discover your greatness, identify and remember your purpose, and live it out to bless the world as only YOU—The One—can.

## NOTE

1. Friedrich Nietzsche, *Aphorisms on Love and Hate.* New York: Penguin, 2015.

Download your **FREE**
*Promise Journal Guide*
& *Promise Process Evaluation* at

jasonhewlett.com/ThePromiseJournalGuide

# INTRODUCTION

---

*Promises are like crying babies in a theater,*
*they should be carried out at once.*

—NORMAN VINCENT PEALE

*This dog will not do his business... I am exhausted*, I mutter to myself as my breath turns into a mist and cloud before me.

We have essentially walked the entire neighborhood, it is snowing and freezing, and we are 45 minutes in.

"Come on pup, you can do this!"

Finally, he squats on some person's yard. Mission accomplished, let's go home!

That's when I realize—I forgot the bag to pick up the mess. I am a 15-minute walk from my house, where the little garbage sacks are.

I have a decision to make: Look to the left, look to the right, and get out of there, or find something to pick up my dog's mess so I can discard it.

As we walk home, I search for one leaf, one newspaper, a fallen tree branch—anything I could find to return and snag that little piece of evidence that proves we were there.

But not one helpful material manifests itself.

As we go bounding up the steps to the house—grateful to finally be home, warm, and out of the elements—I unleash the dog and tell my wife I'll be right back.

Grabbing the baggie, I slip out the door, sprinting in sleet, snow, and slosh back to the scene of the crime. Panting, sweating, I bend over and pick up the mess my dog made, and I dash home.

The bag is full, yet somehow my heart is fuller.

This is the kind of person we strive to be in business, at home, in life, whether anyone knows of our actions or not—the person who has just kept a Promise to do what he knows is right. In the darkness, there is light.

## THIS IS THE PROMISE.

Perhaps you've been on the other end of someone having broken a promise to you.

The previous scenario seems to play out daily in many different realms of life:

- The barefoot walk on the lawn with your infant daughter as she steps in dog poop left behind, consciously, by some inconsiderate family.

- The flooded basement from a dishwasher improperly, quickly, and carelessly installed by a worker in a rush to get to the next job.

- The wife of 39 years left with no money, no job experience, and no options after finding out her husband has been cheating on her and now wants a divorce.

- The salesperson you hired who claimed to be working diligently and following up with your clients but who was actually not making sales and instead taking a free ride.

We all have been victims of someone else breaking a Promise to do what is right in this world, and to be frank, I'm sick of it.

My world has been turned upside down by the careless, thoughtless, selfish actions of others enough that I can stand firmly and say there is no way I'm going to be like that. And it's not a self-righteous declaration, either; it's simply a proclamation to myself that I will make a difference in all that I do, be the best I can be, and follow through on my commitments.

If that very simple concept could seep into the mind of a man in a relationship, a worker in a job, a leader trusted in the community, then the entire world could change.

What is The Promise?

The Promise is simple: It is the highest level of engagement we commit to in any experience.

*The Promise is the highest level of engagement we commit to in any experience.*

A Promise is greater than a goal—it is a sacred commitment.

What are your Promises?

The unbreakables?

The non-negotiables?

You probably haven't really thought about it before; you just naturally make Promises and figure that's just how life is. And in that sense, good for you! You are making a difference.

But what about the subconscious Promises we make, and break, without realizing it?

Such as telling a friend we'll be there and ready for a workout at 6:30 A.M., and the alarm goes off at 6:00 in the morning after you've been up all night with a sick child?

Now it becomes a question of values: Keep a Promise to your friend and show up groggy and dead to the world, potentially damaging your own health even further, but at least you made it! Or keep a Promise to yourself and get some rest.

Not every situation is like this, but there is a give and take. And often the person keeping The Promise—you, The One—is left with the short end of the stick.

When we get right to the heart of discussing why The Promise is so important, it comes down to one thing: When a Promise is broken, there is usually a mess left behind.

Although it may seem juvenile to discuss dog doodoo, the story I opened with is actually the perfect analogy for what happens when Promises are not kept.

It affects everyone.

If you decide to care for yourself and not for others, a Promise is broken.

If you choose to care for others instead of yourself, a Promise has still been broken.

So within that choice, this level of living The Promise-committed lifestyle is wherein lies the character, integrity, and person you truly have become.

This book is not meant to punish, shame, or guilt. However, there will be moments when you will need to stop and ask yourself, "Can I fix what I've done?"

And there will be other times when you'll just have to forgive yourself—or someone else—recommit, and move forward.

Most of all, this book aims to provoke thinking of a higher nature, rather than simply becoming another book of words to read and skim over.

My Promise is to write a book worth reading, that will make you stop and think, and that will encourage you to question your level of integrity.

By no means am I claiming to be on the high horse, yet in the act of writing this book, I am committing to living The Promise at the greatest capacity I can.

I invite you to join me in striving to live fully The Promise.

*When a Promise is broken, there is usually a mess left behind.*

# CHAPTER 1

# CHARACTER

---

*I believe in the sacredness of a promise, that a man's word should be as good as his bond; that character—not wealth or power or position—is of supreme worth.*

—J. D. ROCKEFELLER

What would you give to accomplish your life's one greatest dream?

What if it meant spending your entire life working toward that accomplishment; then suddenly, staring you in the face, is the realization of that dream—that huge Promise you once made to yourself to prove everyone wrong and make something of your talent?

And what if, when the moment came for the realization of your goal, you discover it is morally misaligned with your life's true ambitions?

I had one goal: to headline in Las Vegas.

As an entertainer, I was on my way—and fast.

Having already become one of the top one-man show acts in my state of Utah, building my celebrity, and making all the right connections, I was well on my way. Within three years of beginning my career, I found myself sitting across the table from one of Las Vegas's billionaire hoteliers, who was offering me the fulfillment of my dream.

Let's be fair. It wasn't exactly the whole shebang, not right away at least.

What I was being offered was to have professional managers, producers, writers, and real showbiz legends take over my career, to mentor and mold me into the performer they needed at their soon-to-open mega-hotels.

As my wife and I drove the six-plus hours to Las Vegas in our Subaru Outback from my grandma's second home in Park City, Utah, which we had been renting for three years, we knew this was our dream coming true.

The plan was first to have me go from one casino to another throughout the western United States and perfect my act.

We had seen the shows they had produced, and they were the best between Lake Tahoe, Southern California, and Las Vegas.

They would lock me in for life.

I was to commit my career to their care and tutelage.

The vision was drawn before me: "Your name will be on taxis, on billboards, at the airport, and on the Strip. You just have to listen to our advice, perform what we tell you to, and you will become the next Danny Gans of Las Vegas."

Danny Gans was my hero. A Christian family man working the Strip in his own showroom, making over $100 million on his latest contract. Someone who wasn't a household name, but once you saw him you knew he was the greatest performer you'd ever seen and he became unforgettable.

A clean show. For families. The path was possible!

Yet sitting there with the lawyers and casino brass, my wife and I flipped through the contract and realized a problem: Las Vegas's "family friendly" 1990s theme attempt was no longer what it used to be. In order to make it now, mid 2004, as a non-celebrity in the pre-*America's Got Talent* era, you would need to make your show what had become the new order in Vegas as of 2003:

"What Happens in Vegas Stays in Vegas."

As a boy who grew up in a religious home, very devout to my faith, I was living a standard of morality and integrity and expected the same of the family that I was establishing. Therefore, with this contract I was presented a life-changing decision:

Do the show necessary for me to make it on the Strip and make a windfall of money, become famous, accomplish my dream, or...

Hold my ground.

Significant fear washed over me. I knew this was my moment. I thought there could be future moments—but I knew this was the big one.

This would be the ultimate culmination of everyone telling me throughout my entire life that all of my dreams and goals were unreachable, unattainable—and I would finally be able to tell them where to go.

This was the dream, the Vegas dream, that I had envisioned and worked for and that would set us up for life. I was ecstatic for the change our lives would experience. I knew we would succeed and I would become world-famous at such a young age and stage in my career. I knew my wife could quit her job, we would be secure, and my performing aspirations would be realized.

No more worrying about the next opportunity, if a check might clear, how I would feed my family.

No more answering the doubts and questions of every single person, as I had for years already, regarding my validity, the justification for my hopes. I could just point at a billboard and tell them, "Yes, things have worked out, tickets are only $100 per person if you'd like to come. But good luck getting a ticket—it's sold out every night."

Boom!

This is how it felt. Pure validation, vindication, victory!

And then the reality hit as I realized what I would be trading and what could possibly happen if I fell into the patterns those before me had. From my knowledge of the industry and those enjoying the successes that I knew I would upon performing well, it was apparent I would need to fend off every physical and worldly addiction, habit, and downfall that none who went before me had successfully navigated.

Even if those typical addictions weren't on my radar, they hadn't been on the checklist for my heroes either—and yet they still succumbed.

What of my family? With no children yet, we could create whatever we wanted, whenever we wanted, this new little family of ours.

Yet look at those already performing nightly...not to judge their choices, but it was telling. No one was married to the original spouse with whom they had begun their careers. Few remained in their faith. If the entertainers themselves hadn't fallen into drugs, gambling, and adulterating, their children had grown up with too many luxuries and were ruined for life.

The import of the decision for me was mighty. My wife and I discussed every scenario, excited and fearful, willing and able, yet cautious and worried.

Let's pause for a moment—

## WHAT WOULD YOU DO?

Imagine your in-laws still think your marbles are missing. They love you but are fearful about whether you're going to make it. A legitimate concern!

Imagine that your pipedream career isn't to be and you will eventually be getting a real job...you'd have to!

Imagine your old peers from school asking when you are going to take things seriously and go to college and get your degree like they did.

How about your neighbors and church members asking when you are going to make something of yourself and just keep this hobby thing going as a side deal.

Imagine that your family is still living paycheck to paycheck because you're doing one-off jobs and gigs that are offered on a very inconsistent basis—although you can feel there is momentum in your new career.

Now imagine you have very little income, no health insurance, no home, are renting your grandma's house, and have very few supporters who believe you can make it. And you are sitting in a room with a bunch of Las Vegas producers, managers, and a hotel billionaire who actually believes you can make it!

Writing this now, 15 years after the choice was made, I often wonder what my life would look like had we signed the contract.

Would we be in the same home?

Would we still have our family?

Would I be hoping for an upgrade to first class for my next flight?

Would I have had to cash out a 401(k) just because I had a down year?

Probably not, on all counts.

Yet, when you or I are in the heat of the moment, with a decision to be made, how can we play Monday morning quarterback?

Impossible.

Unless you have made a Promise. A Promise that is unbreakable. Non-negotiable. No matter what.

The Promise for me goes back to high school and the most humiliating moment of my someday hopeful career.

It was the summer before my senior year of high school.

I was so excited.

Having been elected student body president, with an honor roll grade point average (after repeating 9th grade), and a scholarship offer to my dream school for basketball, I'm not sure I could have been much more on top of the world.

But—having discovered I was into singing and dancing at this late date as well—my game plan was changing.

Basketball had been my focus. But after learning what my voice could do as a singer and how my body could express art as a dancer, my life was shifting quickly from athlete on the court to vocal athletics on a stage.

I spent a majority of that summer dancing and singing to my favorite musician's artistry. It was the mid 1990s, and I was a Michael Jackson fanatic.

Back then we had VHS tapes, and I wore out every video I could find of Michael doing his famous dance moves, from the Fred Astaire tap dance, to the Sammy Davis Jr. body contortions, and of course the otherworldly moonwalk.

Subliminally, I made a Promise to myself at some point in time that every waking moment would be spent working on dancing like Michael.

At the time, this actually wasn't a popular thing, as allegations had risen about him that tainted his legacy and damaged not only his own career, but also the lives of the victims.

However, as a teenager, all I wanted to do was figure out how he could move, dance, and perform in such an incredible way. I wanted to dance like Michael.

With the encouragement of neighborhood friends, who got a kick out of my undying practice regimen and ability to mimic, we would drive to the local snow cone stop at the corner grocery store parking lot. My friends would park their cars in a circle, turn the headlights on, crank the MJ music to full blast, and the unsuspecting crowd of teens waiting for their dessert on a summer's night were suddenly gifted a show by a street dancer.

Disclaimer: Utah is not known for street dancers, let alone a street dancer asking for money.

However, money was thrown our way. Yes, even enough for us to go to the movies.

The dollar movies—but still!

What a fun time that was.

I continued my love for musical athleticism by attending a music and dance camp at Brigham Young University. BYU is a religious university owned by The Church of Jesus Christ of Latter-day Saints, of which I am a member.

Attending the BYU Young Ambassadors' camp, I was very excited to meet other like-minded performers and have my chance to showcase what I could do.

When the night of the audition for the talent show arrived, I listened in horror as people, far more talented than I, stood and sang operatic arias that rivaled Broadway—and these were high school kids at a camp!

Backstage I had planned to sing, but hearing the talent level, I knew I could do only one thing to wow the crowd.

I handed the show producer my mixtape, put on my wig, fedora, and sequined glove—and courageously stepped onto the stage that would forever change my life.

As the music boomed, I began to move.

The rhythm and I flowed freely.

I was in my element. This was all I had practiced the entire summer. This was my moment.

The crowd cheered when it became apparent I was pretty good at mimicking Michael's moves.

And then I did a move that Michael was infamous for, and that no young man should do, let alone one at a religious university talent contest audition.

Yes, THAT move!

As I grabbed that area of my body, the crowd went silent…

And then burst into applause!

I was thrilled.

So I did the move again.

More applause and cheering.

My routine was now in full swing—testosterone-induced rage, mixed with artistry that had never been expressed on a real stage with lights. I had found my calling.

As the medley of music came to a close, instead of simply ending with my arms out, as per another signature move of the great MJ, I chose something more dramatic that I had seen him do but had never tried:

Spin—fall to knees—rip off shirt—high-pitched scream—stand—arms out.

The crowd leapt to their feet.

My peers, the attendees, were losing their minds.

Clearly I had received the largest, most impressive ovation of the night and was sure to win the contest the next night for the parents to enjoy.

High-fiving participants were now fearful to take the stage following the complete mopping of the floor with the show that I had done; I was on cloud nine.

Hugs, cheers—they continued.

And then I saw the camp director, the famous and acclaimed leader who had taught us all week.

He wasn't smiling.

I went for the old, "So, what did you think?"—baiting him for the compliment I knew was imminent.

Arms folded, he leaned toward me and said, "Young man, you are disqualified from the talent show."

Stunned, I had no idea why or what he was talking about.

"Why?" I protested. "I just received the best response of the night. In fact, no one has ever done anything as good as that on this stage. I just won the talent contest and it's over."

He looked at me and said with power and authority, "You have been raised to know what is right and what is not. You know the standards of this school. You know who you represent as a man of God. That was the opposite of everything we stand for—and everything you stand for. Just because the audience is cheering and encouraging those types of moves doesn't mean you should do them. You need to choose what type of performer you are going to be. You know better. You are disqualified."

I had never been more incensed.

Everyone else was confused as well. It was just assumed, not only that I would get to be in the talent contest, but that I was going to win it.

Instead, I went back to my room and sat on the bed, shirt torn, sweat dripping from my chest.

I looked across the room at the window, only to see the reflection of myself.

## IN THIS MOMENT I COULD CHOOSE.

Choose whether I was right or he was.

What a jerk! How embarrassing. What does he know?

And I sat there, sulking.

Sad for myself.

Cheated.

And then....

Reflective.

Contemplative.

And quite rapidly it was confirmed in my heart:

He is right.

I know better.

I went too far. I should have never done those moves, even though the crowd was cheering and egging me on.

My parents had asked me not to do those moves when they had caught glimpses of my practicing.

My friends had suggested I may want to strike them from the routine.

But I wanted the performance to be authentic and incredible.

And I made the choice to go for it at that event, and they loved it. And yet, I actually knew better.

Removing my shoes, setting my glasses, hat, wig, and glove on the floor, I reflected on my dream, concerned that I would be shackled my whole life with rules, commandments, and governance of some standard of living that felt completely unreasonable.

But as I thought about it, I realized...maybe those guidelines actually were the best for me to live by and fully commit to. And right then and there, I made a Promise to myself, to the universe, to God, and to my own art that I would never purposefully cross that line again onstage. And that my every move, word, and action would be appropriate for families to enjoy together.

As I write this now, almost 25 years later, it brings tears to my eyes to think that was the very moment that defined my career.

*That was the very moment*
*that defined my career.*


It was the first of many Promises I made to myself—a non-negotiable, something far beyond a mere goal. It was the reason for every choice I've since made, every opportunity turned away, and the reason most people have never heard of me....

And I couldn't be more grateful that in that very moment I made such a Promise to myself.

## WHAT DO YOU STAND FOR?

What offers, opportunities, and promotions have you turned away in order to stick to your guns?

What moments have changed your life because you gave in, succumbed to internal or external pressures, or broke a Promise?

What do you believe in?

If you can't make a Promise and keep it, you very well may succeed in business, and you quite possibly can put on a show, but your soul will be empty.

If you can't make a Promise to yourself and keep it, you will live a life devoid of peace.

The Promise is a choice, a clarion call of character, an investment in integrity.

> *The Promise is a choice,*
> *a clarion call of character,*
> *an investment in integrity.*

Let's conclude where we left off: the Las Vegas choice.

Did I make the choice when I was faced with the opportunity in Las Vegas?

Ultimately, no. It had been made a decade earlier, alone, as a teen, in despair at the edge of my bed following my performance in a Michael Jackson outfit....and then a firm resolve.

It was perhaps a rite of passage, a ritualistic awakening of my heart, and when you go through something so profound and even traumatic, it forges the person you will become and the decisions you make from then on.

As a young boy, I made a Promise to myself that wouldn't be broken, and as a man being handed the golden key to my future, with my wife next to me in a Las Vegas casino and the world's greatest opportunity in front of me, there was no decision to make then and there.

I already knew the answer.

After more back and forth, I told the producers, directors, managers, and owners of what could have been my future, "Thank you, but I'm going to go in a different direction."

I was told I'd never have that opportunity again—and they were right, as I have been blacklisted from headlining in the city.

And that is why few audiences have ever heard of me.

And that is why I can sleep at night.

And that is why you're reading this book.

That is The Promise.

# CHAPTER 2

# IDENTIFY • CLARIFY • MAGNIFY

*Leaders who win the respect of others are the ones who deliver more than they promise, not the ones who promise more than they can deliver.*

—MARK A. CLEMENT

How do you come to your Promise?

Is it a conscious decision that one day you say, "This is me. This is what I stand for. This is what I'm about"?

Most likely—*no*.

Rather, it is a subconscious agreement made between your inner monologue and the character that defines your being.

It is a combination of heart, mind, and yes, soul.

How do we tap into this space?

Simple: We fail enough, or are hurt so often by others, that the fire within us forges metal into mettle. The weapons that have previously damaged our insides now become either our own tool for self-sabotage or our opportunity to fight back.

That's how decisions are made and Promises are created as to who we are, what we will become, and what we will make of this life.

More often than not, we cower to the beast unleashed by disappointment, despair, and especially broken Promises both from ourselves and others.

It is in these moments, when we have tiptoed to the precipice of eternity, our own mortality, that we decide whether to jump into darkness and give up, or fly toward the light and fight back.

Dramatic? Certainly. But what would you expect from a romantic like me?

## WHAT DEFINES YOU?

What makes you the person who will be talked about glowingly or unfavorably upon your departure, not only from the room and latest get-together, but from this short time on earth?

For this reason I love funerals. They're my favorite meetings I attend. Nothing will get you quicker to realizing how short our time is than a funeral, and nothing will help you decide the life you must create in order to live your time well and now.

Combine that with enough attempts at success through failing, which I lovingly called "Failing Frequently" in my previous book, and you will begin to discover and identify the many Promises you must make in this life.

*What will they say when I'm gone?* Big question. Sometimes a sobering answer!

For example, I Promise to be an Artist in every way possible, whether that is music, singing, dancing, comedy, speaking, and even running my business...even though it's oftentimes a bad idea to be too much of an Artist when making business decisions. But when I combine that Promise with my commitment to be a Visionary, it helps me reach new heights.

Does this resonate with you?

If words like Artist and Visionary seem contrived or ridiculous to you, I frankly don't care, because they're The Promises I've made to myself. What I care about is that you figure out yours.

And you can do that through the process I've created to help leaders become Legendary Leaders by discovering their Signature Moves in a simple, life-changing process. And yes, you're a leader, even if you're not in "management."

- IDENTIFY
- CLARIFY
- MAGNIFY

Sounds simple, right?

Maybe, but it will rock your world if you let it work its magic on you.

IDENTIFY • CLARIFY • MAGNIFY is that discovery process we subconsciously go through that helps us end up where we are right this minute. Your life is a result of this process.

Don't believe me?

How much money do you have?

What's your job situation look like?

How about your family life?

All of it has manifested a certain way because of the process.

Throw in some of life's curveballs—a.k.a., challenges and unforeseen struggles—and that is your life! Okay, maybe you're a victim of something very tragic, and if so, I'm sorry to hear that. But honestly—be honest now—you mostly created all that you are and all that you have!

Success or Failure—it's on you.

What can you do about it now?

Make a conscious choice at this moment in time to direct the outcome with the process and The Promise.[1]

Example: I IDENTIFY in myself that I am an Artist. That happened when I was very young. It wasn't until others helped me CLARIFY that it was a true and real fact—and eventually even came along on the journey with me and helped—that I was able to take the next step, whereby I MAGNIFY my Promise to utilize that which I IDENTIFY as.

## IDENTIFY

I am an Artist. And so I live every day in a way that allows me to do my Art, even when I don't know if anyone will accept it or even cares about what is being created.

Example: I've been on the board for the Hale Centre Theatre in Sandy, Utah, which is easily America's finest wholesome entertainment venue for families, for eight years. Recently, I attended a board meeting in which one by one, pillars of the community—business leaders who have their names on the largest buildings in the state, legends of our time who I wished knew my name—walked up to me, shook my hand or gave me a hug, and told me how much they enjoy my blog and writing.

I was confused.

They never comment on a post. They never respond to my writings. Yet here they were, praising my work and describing it in detail as to what they liked! They were even claiming that they share it in team meetings at work and in family gatherings with their children.

What? They've never inquired about hiring my services as a speaker and they're loving my blog? I was stunned.

Background as to my surprise: I have written a blog faithfully for nearly a decade. Only in the past three years have I dedicated a majority of it to The Promise as a concept.

It arrives in the reader's inbox on Sunday mornings, every single week, no matter what. That, in and of itself, is a Promise!

To be perfectly honest, on average I receive four comments per post! Four!!!!!!!!

The only time it's higher than four is when I reply to each comment; then it becomes eight.

Can you understand why I was floored to hear so many business leaders are reading and loving my blog?

And yet, I don't write it for the comments. Heck, if no one read it, I'd still write it! Because I'm an Artist! That's my Promise!

Frankly, comments are nice, when they're actually nice and encouraging, but that's not the reason I write. If it were, I'd have given up years ago! Instead, I just create Art that I figure must either be for me only—and no one else cares—or for the four people who comment, or for the people who will find it when I'm dead and say, "Oh, that's nice. I wish I could have commented on his blog and encouraged his writing before he died. Oh well."

What you IDENTIFY as your traits, gifts, talents, skills—that is who you are. And to share them is your Promise.

Unfortunately, we are in search of approval, thumbs up, and standing ovations...and when we don't get them, we give up!

But I'm an ARTIST! Show me you love me!

I've done too much homework to know full well that the most incredible artists who ever lived were rarely beloved in their time. My goodness, just look at Vincent van Gogh's story.

Vincent van Gogh was shunned his entire life for his perception of the world and translation of what he saw, which became his Art. He was made fun of, despised, even put in a mental institution. Traveling from town to town, he ended up a drunk, cut off his ear to express his love and sorrow, and was completely misunderstood during his short existence.

It wasn't until he was dead—literally, dead—that he had his first art show, with his masterpieces surrounding his corpse at his funeral as people viewed his art and shopped.

I don't know what's more insane! Him or that funeral story!

And that is something I IDENTIFY with as well. So if someone reads this book and comments, then I'M THRILLED! And if they hate it, I don't care! I'm an Artist. That's my Promise.

So, I ask you again, what is your Promise?

## EXERCISE: IDENTIFY

Take a minute to do this exercise, which you maybe did one time when you were a kid but never thought about again.

Instead of pinpointing one word that makes up your Signature Move—your distinct, one and only thing that makes up your very being—instead of that daunting task, do this:

Go for 100.

Write up to 100 of your gifts, talents, skills, traits—be it nouns, verbs, adjectives...whatever you need to do to write. But you need to IDENTIFY yourself.

Don't edit—just write as fast as possible.

The first time I tried this, I got to 34 characteristics and couldn't think of one more.

And then I looked at the 34. And I discovered deeper meaning to each one.

For example, if I write a list of things I IDENTIFY with that make up who I am, words that easily come to mind are:

- Funny
- Careful

- Proactive

- Entertaining

- Energetic

Let's dissect one of those words: entertaining.

That could mean a whole lot of things, and it opens up more options if I dig deeper, such as:

- Musical

- Satirist

- Impressionist

- Author

- Speaker

- Storyteller

- Embellisher

- Performer

- Producer

- Actor

- Singer

Does this make sense?

Imagine giving yourself this gift of character introspection and mindful self-examination! It is freeing, moving, and will set your life in motion from this time forth.

Most will read right over this portion and not do the exercise, but those who stop even for five minutes and try it will receive profound results that can transform their lives immediately.

I'll never forget taking a young accountant I was coaching through this process. He struggled to get even a few traits written down. I pressed him to find more and to dissect the ones he had already listed.

He then had an epiphany right in front of me: He was a Performer, wanted to make people laugh, but wanted to move them with his music as well. It was something he'd done in the past but had hidden away in order to make a living.

Why was he in accounting? Because he was good at it, went to school for it, and his parents had told him it would be a good and steady paycheck! All good reasons, but not good enough once he realized his true identity through the IDENTIFY process.

He quickly quit his job and began the new process of defining his Artistry. Now he is performing on cruise ships worldwide and has created the life he always dreamed of having, subconsciously, from his cubicle as an accountant.

This is not to say that one life is better than the other; it's simply to qualify why this process is so profound and will change your life as soon as you're willing to do it.

A word of caution: If you discover in your IDENTIFY exercise that you should run away with the circus and yet you have a family to feed and a job that pays the bills, PLEASE don't just drop everything and do that. Discuss it with your family, see if there's an option for an exit strategy from your current employment situation, and realize equally that you can IDENTIFY skills that can become your new and once-forgotten hobby without having to throw away responsibilities to make it your job.

Your Promise to yourself is to live and share what you are—what you IDENTIFY as being your true self—and to bless the world as only you can with your amazing gifts, a.k.a., your Signature Moves.

Once you've gone through this process of IDENTIFYING the 100, now circle those words that really resonate with you, and whittle the list down to your TOP 10 most important qualities—words that make you who you are, that you could be happy having listed in your final description of your life and life's work when friends, family, and strangers attend your funeral.

In my Top 10, some of my words are:

- Entertainer

- Family Man

- Integrity

- Connector

What are yours? Take the time to do this exercise, and truly, your life will never be the same.

## CLARIFY

Armed with your Top 10 IDENTIFY List from the previous exercise—those gifts, talents, traits, and skills you feel make you who you are—you're ready to move to the next step. Put that list aside and forget about it for a moment.

As you bravely move into the world of CLARIFY, this is your chance to consider what others have to say about you and your abilities.

Don't be deterred by this step, as it is perhaps the most challenging—and fascinating—part of the whole assignment.

Even the greatest artists and legends in history have gone through this CLARIFY process, whether they liked it or not.

For example, Reginald Dwight was forced by his parents to learn classical piano. Growing up in England, he had little choice, but once in a while he could hear the radio playing the music he loved: music from America by Elvis Presley, Fats Domino, Chuck Berry—real Rock n' Roll!

And then four boys from Liverpool took the world by storm with their music. The Beatles became world-famous and motivated Reginald further to improve his singing and songwriting.

As a teenager, Reg entered his original songs into a local contest... only to be told the following: "Young man, you're a very good singer, a wonderful piano player, and you write beautiful melodies, but these lyrics are atrocious. You need someone to write the words for you!"

Luckily another boy, named Bernie Taupin, had submitted his poems of fanciful lyrics, yet had no one who could put music to them.

Paired together, Reg and Bernie began creating music with the talents both displayed. Eventually, they also realized Reginald Dwight wasn't the best name for a Rock n' Roll artist, so they borrowed names from band members and thus was born: ELTON JOHN!

This story is awesome because a young Elton (Reginald) was told he was good at certain things but not at others, and this made all the difference in CLARIFYING his life's work and what was necessary for him to succeed. He needed a writing partner, and Bernie helped complete one of music history's most legendary duos.

How do we accept the criticisms and judgments of others? What I love about this story as well is that the judges were helpful in finding a solution, which isn't always the case.

As you consider what people in your life have told you about your talents, what has been said and what has stuck out?

Think of words your teachers wrote on report cards or at the top of an essay, encouraging you to continue one way or recommending you find another. Perhaps your peers had a hand in giving you suggestions as to how amazing your talents and natural gifts are. So often we just brush encouragement off as a little compliment that means nothing, when in reality it could be the very words needed to lift you to a new level.

As the loudest, most talkative kid in the school, I became known as the kid with the big mouth. It wasn't until I went to the dentist that I realized this was actually a good thing. My dentist told me it was great I had a big mouth (a literal one!), pointed out I seemed to have more control over my facial muscles than others, and even noticed I could imitate the sounds in the dentist's office, and he got a kick out of it.

This was the beginning of my CLARIFY process, realizing that it was okay to be me (unique, quirky, doing voices and sounds, making faces) and that it even entertained someone else. Soon the same things made my friends laugh. Now I was going through the process naturally of IDENTIFY • CLARIFY • MAGNIFY!

By the time I was halfway through high school, I figured I would be headed to the NBA to become a professional basketball player—at least that was my dream.

With a letterman jacket showcasing my accolades, I walked down the halls singing my heart out because I was happy, confident, and knew my path.

My best friend, Quinn Dietlein, had recently told me that I had an incredible singing voice as I imitated him doing his vocal warm-ups, and with his encouragement, I started singing everywhere.

As I belted out "The Lion Sleeps Tonight" in the halls of our small private school, suddenly the door to the music room flew open and there was the choir teacher, Mrs. Rosalind Hall, singing back at me as if we were doing a duet.

She asked, in her singing voice, "Who's singing in the hall!!!!?"

I stopped and said, "Me. I'm sorry. I'll stop," as I figured I was in trouble.

She continued, singing away while speaking, like in an opera, "Why aren't you in the choir!!!!???"

I said, "Oh, I don't sing. I play basketball. I'll stop now."

She demanded, "Come into my classroom!" in her Welsh accent and full voice.

Entering her classroom, I was not sure what was going on, but she told me this was my audition. For the choir. She said they were in need of male singers and she could tell I was a singer.

I assured her I wasn't a singer but that I could imitate voices.

She said, "Prove it!"

So I sang "Alvin & The Chipmunks Christmas Song" in their voices.

She looked at me curiously, eyebrows raised, and said, "Young man, that's not normal." And then she laughed.

Then she said, "YOU ARE A SINGER! No one can do that voice; it's not even a real voice. What else can you do with your voice?"

That's when she discovered I had quite the range, as in multiple octaves, no break to falsetto. Her eyes grew big upon hearing what I was capable of with no training. She then prophesied:

"You will be a Singer! You will be on stages around the world! Your voice is astounding. I will teach you!"

And I became her mentee, as she pulled me from classes she felt I didn't need and put me in choirs and music classes that she knew would accelerate my abilities.

How grateful I am for Mrs. Hall, that she made a Promise subconsciously to burst into the hall and "discover" anyone singing. How grateful I am that she CLARIFIED my talents, for I just thought they were silly and pointless, whereas she knew they were unique and extraordinary.

She was my CLARIFY moment, along with my dentist who CLARIFIED that my big mouth and facial muscles enabled me to make funny sounds. Now here I am decades later, and I have made a living with this big mouth that sings, speaks, and performs all over the world!

Your turn—

# EXERCISE: CLARIFY

Take a moment to consider what others have told you are your gifts and talents. Write them down.

If you can't think of any or want more clarity, it is time to reach out to those you trust, be it family, friends, teachers, employers, etc. Tell them you are doing a project to clarify your talents and ask them what they'd say are your gifts and even your Signature Moves.

When you receive the responses, along with all you can remember others have said through the years, now it is time to take your IDENTIFY list and TOP 10 back out to compare and contrast.

You're about to be stunned.

A majority of what you IDENTIFY for yourself is going to match up with what others have CLARIFIED about you! And what's even more amazing is the words they used compared to yours.

For example, if I say I IDENTIFY myself as "Funny," they will CLARIFY that I'm "Hilarious." Better word! Or if I say I'm "Entertaining," they'll say I'm "Inspiring." I like both!

Imagine getting these words back from those who know you best. It's incredible and will change your life and the words you believe about yourself.

Better yet, this will give you words and ideas, talents and gifts, that you would NEVER have considered, but that others see in you. For example, when I did this exercise with my wife, she gave me words like: "Considerate," "Faithful," and "Thoughtful."

Wow! I love that!

Now these words become known as your Signature Moves, as they are from you but also confirmed by others. They are what you become known for, they are what others expect from you, and they drive your entire life's work.

What are your Signature Moves?

Are you ready to do this exercise? Because as you CLARIFY that which makes you who you are in the eyes of the world, you now have the chance to make and keep even more powerful Promises in living what has been said.

Which brings us to the final step—

## MAGNIFY

With your list of IDENTIFY traits, combined with the CLARIFY list from others you know and trust, now you have the words and courage to move to the final step: MAGNIFY.

MAGNIFY is the hardest part of the process, and it is the reason for this book.

When we realize what we are made of and what others see we are capable of, it is now time to Promise to take it to the world. Here are the steps within MAGNIFY:

- Own It!

- Leverage It!

- Teach & Share It!

Sounds simple...yes. But how often do people have incredible talents and gifts that are hidden from the world? All the time.

Are you one of these people?

The Promise gives you the blueprint as to how you can make and keep The Promise to The One who will bless the world as only you can.

If you make The Promise and don't keep your end of the bargain, you are just like everyone else. Broken Promises abound the world over. With the exception of pure accidents, they are the reason for everything sad you see on the news and most of the bad that has happened in your life and family. Broken Promises are what halt the progression of mankind.

Don't contribute to that mess.

You have your lists, your words, you have an IDENTITY and CLARITY—now go out and MAGNIFY it. And when you do, the world will take notice. If you've broken Promises up until now, this is your moment to say, "I'm now a Promise Maker & Keeper. My word and my life are my Promise."

The following chapters will outline how you can embrace this philosophy, becoming a Promise Messenger while you Own that which makes you the wonderful person you are, Leverage what great gifts you have to enhance your life and the lives of others, and then rightfully Teach & Share that which you become.

## EXERCISE: MAGNIFY

Your exercise is to determine your Signature Moves and now make and keep The Promise in bringing them to the world. This book will show you how.

Welcome to The Promise!

## NOTE

1. For a detailed example of what this process might look like in your Promise Journal, download your free Promise Process Evaluation guide at jasonhewlett.com/ThePromiseJournalGuide.

# CHAPTER 3

# INTEGRITY

---

*I believe keeping our promises
should be our highest priority.*

—TOM COBURN

Take a moment to consider the thoughts running through your mind when you casually open a social media platform to share something with your audience, either from your phone, laptop, or tablet. You know perhaps 100 people will see it—your closest friends, family, and even some of their followers.

You're about to post something a bit provocative. Not suggestive, but with the intention of pressing some buttons. Yes, this is a post about your opinions, or a story, or maybe your spin on an experience.

It's late at night. You know that once you click "Post" you will put the electronics away and awaken the next morning to some comments from those who saw it, because it is certainly too good not to comment on.

You sleep soundly, self-assured that what you posted is good and needed to be shared, and life goes on.

Now, imagine for a moment that as you write, instead of just your family and maybe 100 or more people seeing it, you know that once you press "Post" over 100 million people will read, see, or hear it over the next three days as it spreads like wildfire around the world.

How different would your writing be? What would you hold back? What would you add?

Had I known this was going to happen, I would have changed...

This happened to me the night I got in bed and posted about seeing my wife at Target, a store just down the street from our home, as I casually shared an insight I'd had while shopping there.

I figured a few hundred people might see it and would think it was cute. Little did I know that within 48 hours we would be the main headline in news stories around the world, upstaging the Kardashians the day Kim and Kanye West had their first baby and trending as the top name on the planet for my 15 minutes of viral fame.

How different would my post have been had I known this was going to happen?

Pretty interesting to think about!

Truth is, I would have chosen to use a few words and phrases differently for sure, but the ones I chose, assuming few were watching or looking, made the post as magical as it was.

Integrity is doing what you know is right whether anyone is watching or not.

*Integrity is doing
what you know is right
whether anyone is watching or not.*

I'll share the post in a minute, and if you haven't read it before just ask your mom, wife, or girlfriend, and it is almost a guarantee they'll recall either hearing about it, reading it, sharing it, loving it, or completely hating it.

There was no in-between on this post, and there is no in-between with Integrity.

What is Integrity and your Promise in having this crucial trait?

Think of it this way: You're on a diet. You have sworn off sugar, white breads, and bad carbs, and you're starting to really regret that whole fun commitment as you arrive at the Sunday Super Bowl party with friends.

Drinks filled with sugar surround you, as well as candy, popcorn, nachos, pizza—the whole nine yards.

What have you committed to? You made a Promise to yourself not to indulge. Sadly, your timing was off and you forgot this big party was this weekend.

Your self-discipline is waning. You are about to crash.

What is Integrity?

You made a Promise to yourself not to eat it. Maybe you even told your family and perhaps a friend who is at the party.

Let's say those people are there and they are watching.

Integrity says you keep your commitment and don't eat anything and merely suffer through it.

Lack of discipline says you sneak off in the corner and eat some of the goodies, hoping no one is watching.

Lack of Integrity says you tell yourself it never happened.

Now let's say none of your friends or family are there, and there is no one who knows the Promise you made to yourself. Are you off the hook?

It depends on your level of Integrity.

Same with business dealings—time spent working versus time spent surfing the Internet saying you're working.

Collecting a paycheck for all that surf time?

Recently I was asked by the School Board of Education to film, edit, and create a program for kids heading to college.

I told them I'd do it for free but that we would need some funds in order to hire the film crew, editors, and buy stock photos and videos to supplement the project.

Since I was in charge of the entire project, the payment came through my office and was made out to my business.

In full disclosure, much of the stock footage was already in our possession from other projects, and the film crew and editors owed me many hours of time for other things we had worked on previously.

The crew wasn't expecting payment no matter how long the filming took. The editor wasn't expecting payment no matter how long the edits required.

The payment came through my office. No one but me and the client knew how much I had received.

What is Integrity?

I had secured the funds for editing, filming, and stock footage.

I had a choice...but when it comes to The Promise of Integrity, did I really?

Not if I live The Promise.

Instead, I requested more edits than were needed and returned a beyond-A+ product to the client. They received far more than they paid for. I spent over one week's worth of my own valuable time editing, outlining, and directing how the program should look, while pushing my editing team to the point where they said, "We have gone beyond the amount of time owed to us. This is becoming too much."

To which I said, "You're getting paid. I received funding from the client. Keep pushing, keep going—it will be worth it."

And we over-delivered to the client. We sent a product that should be used for decades to come. It is beautiful, 100 percent amazing.

And I sent the entire allotment of funds to the filming and editing team.

I didn't keep a penny, even though I did tens of thousands of dollars of work in my time spent.

My decision went beyond self-discipline or self-control; it was a matter of Integrity and Promise to Self—something I could either keep or break.

Truth is, we all struggle with this to some extent or another.

Judgments from peers and family can keep us strong for so long, but it's when we are alone, in the darkness of our natural tendencies and habits, that we really find out what we're made of.

Most of us, in these moments, fall and fail—big-time.

Think of the last time you said you'd do something for free and, once in the trenches, realized you made a mistake. You committed too much. Your first thought is:

How do I get out of this?

The person of Integrity still fulfills the agreement.

If you bail early, you will forever be tainted by your miscalculation and unwillingness to keep your Promise.

This happened to me with a mastermind group.

I was so excited to become a part of it. They vetted me, quizzed me, and questioned my commitment. I said all the right things. I was accepted into the group.

And then, the very first call, I was traveling and realized, with the change of time zones, that I had messed up the phone call time, which would conflict with my own flight.

I remember calling in and admitting my mistake and how embarrassed I was, and I promised that it wouldn't happen again. I told them I'd hang on the call as long as I could before my flight took off.

When I finished speaking, I guess they figured I'd hung up rather than stayed on the line, so the group—my peers—began talking about how I wasn't the right fit, that I had broken a Promise to them, and that if I was really all in I would never have made the mistake and even stayed off the flight to be on the call.

I remember realizing that they were right, and also that I didn't want to be in this group. I felt terrible and guilty. I had compromised my word, and I was already committed to be in this mastermind!

All I could do was compose an e-mail asking their forgiveness and bow out. It was humiliating. It was a brutal display of my lack of Integrity. I could have hung in there and suffered through this group's calls from then on, but instead my Integrity took a complete blow on my first engagement with them and those people will never see me the same way again.

I broke a Promise to them by accepting the place in their group initially, when I knew the time commitment required would be too much, and then I broke a Promise to be on the first call. My Integrity was in question, and I put the final stamp on the envelope sealing my lack of it when I left the group. Essentially, I was dead in the water.

It is one thing to break a Promise to peers and friends, with the humiliation and embarrassment of not being what they thought you were, but it's quite another to face the reality that you broke a Promise to yourself.

When we can't keep a Promise to ourselves, we are guilty of missing the mark. It is in these moments—when a commitment is too difficult to keep despite what we've promised ourselves and others we will do—that we need to decide what kind of person we are.

If Promise-breaking and a lack of Integrity weren't symptomatic of the most chronic illness of society and the greatest challenge we all face, there would be no need for this book.

Yet relationships are built upon this thing called Integrity—that is, ultimately, Trust—and can crumble in one moment of weakness, with a Promise made and broken due to a lack of Integrity.

The same can be said in business, in money, in health—you name it. Integrity is the name of the Promise game.

Integrity is a buzzword tacked onto leadership courses and ethics programs, yet how often are we really assessing our own values unless someone calls us on it?

Recently, I received a request for a speaking engagement. A wonderful call with the potential client ensued. I quoted my speaking fee, which I knew would be quite high for this particular group and their industry, and even suggested that perhaps we should negotiate a "local fee" to make it more feasible.

The client was thrilled and said they could work with that but not with the higher fee.

And then I never heard back.

A few weeks went by, and my e-mails and calls were ignored.

Then, out of nowhere, I woke up one morning to a harshly worded e-mail from the client:

"I discussed your fee with my boss. Come to find out, you spoke at his brother's company two years ago for half of the discounted fee quote you gave me. If you will give us the discount you gave them, we are ready to confirm."

I was stunned. I wondered if I had made a mistake in doing the event two years earlier. She was calling me out for something that contractually the former client wasn't supposed to divulge.

And then I realized the truth of the matter. When beginning my speaking career, I quoted a certain fee in the hopes of receiving it, but often I had to discount it in order to get any opportunity to prove my worth onstage. In this instance, it was for a group that could showcase my skills to numerous businesses, and so I was willing to discount it heavily as a marketing opportunity.

I returned to the potential client and acknowledged that yes, we had done it for that fee, and that yes, that was an incredible price for what is offered. And then I spelled out the reasoning for doing so, such as marketing as well as just beginning my career as a speaker to prove myself.

I said firmly, "Here we are, two years later. I have now spoken to audiences all over the world for the fees we quote to everyone. I perhaps shouldn't have even offered a local discount to you; however, I'm happy to honor it, but I can in no way do it for the fee from a few years ago when I began my career. If this doesn't work for you at this time, then I'm happy to work with you when that fee is within budget."

She responded quickly, saying she respected my reasoning for offering the former fee and also understood that I was still giving her a special opportunity with the local fee as currently constituted. She said she would get right back to me with an answer from her employer.

Yet again, she ghosted me. After I finally got a hold of her, she said she could pay only what I had received from the other company, so the deal was dead.

In this exchange, I could easily have feigned ignorance or made something up, even offered her a further discount on my work. If I had done that, I might have put into question my worth and devalued the higher fees recently paid by national and local clients. Instead, I was willing to walk away from an offer I would have liked to have confirmed right away, because I needed the work at the time of year she was offering it. I would rather sit home working in full Integrity than sell myself at a lower price to gain a short-term reward.

Integrity is your moral compass, your values defined. It comes into question most often when people have a hard time believing you're actually who you say you are to their face when you're behind closed doors.

To say I feel confident writing about this topic is questionable—not because I lack knowledge about and experience with it, but rather because of the potential for human error that might impact my credibility. Every day I fear the slip-up that may jar a lifetime of working to build Integrity, when in any one moment it could collapse all around me with one lapse of judgment.

Yet when we live with Integrity—when we make the daily choice to keep The Promise to Self to live with honor—we have nothing to hide, or to be ashamed of, along life's great journey—even a mistake.

Perfection is not attainable; that isn't what we are shooting for. It's about going all in and doing all we can to keep the Promise when we've made one. Plain and simple.

Years ago, I announced that I would be writing this book.

I told myself daily that I was working on it. I told my peers I was working on it!

I lied to myself every day and went to bed every night devastated by my lack of Integrity.

Sure, I had every excuse imaginable: life gets in the way, money is tight, kids need attention, health is neglected. It's a vicious cycle.

But what of Integrity? What of saying to yourself you're going to do something, and then telling yourself you're doing it, and then realizing you're eating a donut in the corner closet at the Super Bowl Party and telling yourself, or others, that you're not!?

We can laugh about it now, but in reality, it's no laughing matter.

## INTEGRITY IS ACTIVELY KEEPING YOUR PROMISE.

So what are your Promises that make up your Integrity?

What are you doing in the presence of no one but yourself that is making you a better person, someone who contributes to the world, or, in contrast, that causes you to keep breaking Promises to yourself and those who mean the most to you?

When the life I appear to live is congruent with the life I actually live—the life that no one else sees—that is fulfillment, peace, strength, and Integrity.

It is the same as when you hear a group of beautiful singers harmonizing. They sound incredible, and your ears relish the euphony of their tone and creativity as they align every note together. It is stunning.

Yet if one person loses their place or misses a note, even while still singing the words correctly, any ear can hear when the harmony breaks apart. It's a dissonance that's undeniable.

And it rattles the soul of the listener. It's so bad and painful that you squint in agony.

That is what is happening in your heart when you pretend to live one way online or in public and are inconsistent in private.

## INTEGRITY IS YOUR HARMONY.

All of us struggle with this, so don't be discouraged. Just quickly make up your mind that what you say you'll do and what you actually do, and who you say you are and who you actually are, both to others and to yourself, are in alignment. When they align, you will find absolute clarity, joy, peace, fulfillment, and harmony in this life.

If at work you are Superman, catering to everyone's needs, the greatest performer, and the most patient, empathetic, loving, and helpful person the workplace has ever seen, and then you come home and become the Incredible Hulk, filled with rage, anger, and impatience...there is no Integrity there. And eventually, your heroic persona at work will break too.

Which are you?

Integrity is having all worlds align. It is congruence on and off the stage. And it is the greatest challenge of life.

What is the answer?

How can you capture or reclaim your Integrity?

## EXERCISE: INTEGRITY

Here's a quick exercise:

Look at your calendar from the last few days or week.

Of your to-do lists and needs between home and work, which did you say you did and which did you really do? If you've told yourself you did something, such as finished a project or read the kids a book before bed at night, did you actually finish the project or just dial it in to get it over with? Did you really read the book or walk upstairs and realize the child was asleep and returned to bed, telling your spouse it was a great read?

This isn't an exercise to make you feel bad; it's meant to call into question your level of Integrity and The Promise that you want to live in this life.

Next level of the exercise:

Open your journal and read what you were doing and thinking one year ago. If you're struggling with the same things today as you were back then, you have some recommitting to do.

Now just write out those Promises with clear definitions.

Say you realize that you still owe the same amount on the house today as you did a year ago, only having paid interest, while you had committed to begin paying down the principal. You have overspent elsewhere. This is a normal occurrence, but at the same time, it is a broken Promise to yourself.

Write a new commitment: *Today I will set up an automatic payment of $50 extra going toward our mortgage.* As simple and small as that is, it's a Promise fulfilled and moves the needle of your life immediately.

Maybe you see the same weight on the scale today as you weighed one year ago, or worse yet, you've gained pounds!

Write a new commitment: *I've had it! I'm working out three times this week and waking up thirty minutes earlier. And no more donuts in the closet...*

Better yet: *I am healthy, which means I feed my body the healthiest nutrients, I sweat daily as I enjoy nature, and I treat my body like it is my Temple.*

Now that's a Promise!

This Integrity Promise Exercise is very easy. It may be depressing when you see what you lied about to yourself, when you discover that you didn't accomplish something you thought you had, or when you realize how little has improved from where you were a year ago, but that's why we are doing this.

*There is no point in reading any book in the history of the world if it doesn't change your thinking and behavior.*

Honestly, there is no point in reading any book in the history of the world if it doesn't change your thinking and behavior. If this book isn't for you, then give it to someone else.

I believe you know I'm speaking to your core and true inner self, that voice inside that says, "Dang, he's right! What's the deal with my progress? I have to do something to be better."

Now you're bummed. That's okay. Get over it, and get moving. Change is painful and tough, yet it will also be extremely empowering!

*Change is painful and tough, yet it will also be extremely empowering!*

You'll make Promises fast—make it so they are attainable. Don't set lofty goals that will be once written, never achieved—plans that become merely the dreams of last year when you glance at them again down the road.

This becomes your new blueprint!

If you don't have a journal to peruse from last year (and if I may, I highly recommend that you begin keeping a journal for a few reasons, such as therapy and gratitude, but even just to keep track of life's events as we're discussing here), then look at your Google

Calendar, or your Franklin Planner, or scroll through some photos and see your life from a third-party perspective.

And make some new Promises to be consistent.

## THAT IS THE SECRET OF THE PROMISE: CONSISTENCY.

And Consistency in keeping a Promise—that is Integrity at its highest level.

So now, we return to the post online, on your social media page, that which you think only 100 family and friends will read... but then, what? One hundred million people read it instead.

What do you write differently? How is your perspective altered? Perhaps a few words, thoughts, and descriptions change. That's fine. But is the essence of what you were going to say still there?

That is The Promise. That is Integrity. Create as if no one is looking, and then still create even when everyone is commenting, for good or bad. Trust me, the bad gets ugly at those numbers. Don't back down. Keep at it. Keep your Promise! Keep going!

*Create as if*
*no one is looking.*

Here's what I wrote on Facebook that fateful evening:

December 1, 2015

Kind of embarrassed to admit this, but I think I sort of cheated on my wife today.

To explain what I mean, I was at Target getting a few manly things, you know—eyebrow tweezers, toenail clippers, beard trimmers, mustache molding waxes, some beef jerky, sardines, trail mix, a loofah—and as I went to pay I saw this woman in line that knocked me out.

I thought, "Wow, some lucky guy is with her," and in a split second I realized it was my wife!

You know, it was just out of context to see my spouse at the same store, in the same line, living her life and not knowing she might be at the same place, same time, different car.

There was a person between us, so I just watched my cute little Love, tried to text her stuff like, "Hey Hottie" and "What are you buying now my Babelicious?," none of which got her attention as she was looking for a coupon she'd saved just for this purchase.

So I gave up getting her attention, as you can imagine I easily could have humiliated her by leaping on the register as a Raptor and really making her publicly proud, and instead just stood back and silently observed my feelings about this woman.

First off, I was taken aback by how amazingly beautiful she is once again. I believe I see it often, but today, not knowing she was at the store, I saw her with new eyes and just couldn't believe I get to be her fella.

It made me blush—but no one could see it under my huge monster Movember beard.

Second, it amazed me that she didn't notice me in the slightest. This is both a good and a bad thing. Good in that she doesn't have a wandering eye. Good in that she didn't see the creepy dude with the overgrown mink on his face peering over her shoulder. But maybe that's bad, too, like what if it hadn't been me? I need to get her another can of mace just in case.

But it was also bad because I realized how close I came to not ever winning her love in the first place, and the herculean efforts I had to make all those years ago to even get her attention just to say yes to one date!

For a minute I felt that familiar grief of doom when I first saw her and knew well, that's impossible. But somehow I nabbed her despite my insecurities, inabilities, and imperfections.

Third, I was ultimately so pleased to see her in complete confidence on this day, as the independent, capable, humble, fun, sweet, kind, awesome person she is.

And then she grabbed her things and walked out the door.

I never said anything, didn't flag her down, just watched her walk away, admiringly, knowing she's my wife and I love everything about this woman.

She rarely looks at Facebook so she won't see this post, she won't realize she was kind of cheated on today, but I thought I'd share with you all since I'm just a dweeby guy making my way through life, and at the same time sure there are those who have had the same experiences regarding their loved ones in one way or another, and these moments are perfect.

Lesson of the Day: It's good to look at those we love with fresh eyes whenever we can to remind us how lucky we are to have their light in our lives.

Did you catch some of the phrases I maybe wanted to change? Some of the contradictory statements? If you didn't find them, just google the post and it will come up with all the good, the bad, and the ugly that others said. It's fascinating, and equally disturbing, to read what everyone thought about it.

But what does this have to do with Integrity?

It was a call-out to click bait. Totally!

It was a clarion call to men to be faithful to their spouse. Boom!

It was an invitation to those who no longer appreciate people they see on a daily basis to realize that they are a gift and should be treated and viewed as such. Oh yeah!

For a few weeks I was called the Man of Every Woman's Dreams.

And I was despised by every man I met for writing such ridiculousness.

It is hilarious how everyone saw this post so differently.

But there were some men who loved it, other women who hated it, and few in between.

What it comes down to is the fact that every reader who clicked on it assumed I was confessing to cheating on my wife, enticed by the fruit of the tree and then quickly taken aback by the sweetness of the truth of the post in its resolution.

A Love Story.

Man sees wife—falls in love all over again. Even though I was never out of love, it was just reaffirmed in a new way that very day.

This is the story that launched The Promise. After years of my sharing funny routines, music and parodies, the voices of others that I could imitate—which helped make me a living, but which, in video form, were barely shared online—this post, in my own voice, my own words, unedited, unbridled, and completely authentic, launched The Promise as a concept I teach worldwide.

It was a call-out to personal Integrity.

It was the first of anything I had created that received worldwide attention and was shared like a virus for all that is good and bad of that type of sharing.

This post was pure vulnerability, comically me, self-effacing, and yet grateful and assured. This was the closest to Integrity I had ever come in writing or public speaking.

## WHAT IS YOUR TRUE VOICE?
## YOUR TRUE GIFT? YOUR IDENTITY?

We discussed in the last chapter how to discover it, embrace it, and accept it in yourself. The sooner you do so, the quicker that peace, comfort, and joy will fill your life.

Remember: Integrity. It is your character, morality, Identity, and choices all wrapped into one. You either have it or you don't. If you've lost it or never had it, decide today to make a Promise and keep it, and see how quickly your life changes.

# CHAPTER 4

# SELF-ACCEPTANCE

*I feel keeping a promise to yourself is a
direct reflection of the love you have for yourself.*

—STEVE MARABOLI

Remember the first day of school? Facing those people? The smell of your kindergarten room, the wonder and amazement of the huge school, the feeling you had of being all grown up—all five or six years of yourself?

I was five. My parents started me a few months early, as they figured I was ready.

That first school bus ride was quite the eye opener.

I walked on to find only a few people in the very back. Confidently walking up to an older kid, I said, "I want to sit back here with you because you're cool."

The guy looked back at me. He was a bit larger than I was, but you don't notice that when you're a kid. And he said, "You're just a kid. Why do you want to sit back here? Hey man, your mouth is huge!"

This was my first interaction on a school bus as a five-year-old. Come to find out, this was a high school football star, the ultimate jock, and he was my first bully.

But instead of being mean back to him, I acknowledged that yes, I did have a big mouth, so I opened it as big as I could to make him laugh.

Laugh he did! As did a few others. As did everyone who entered the bus over the next 45 minutes as we drove through neighborhoods and said jock showed off his young seatmate. I proudly sat beside him all the way to school, with him tapping my shoulder to do that thing again with my mouth and me proudly displaying and opening my mouth as wide as possible for all to see.

Laughs abounded. Laughs continued throughout the first day of school. I became known quite quickly as:

The Kid with The Big Mouth

Everyone was telling me to "Open your mouth!" and then they'd run off laughing.

By the end of the school day, my Mom asked, "How was school? Was it fun?"

I said, "I don't like school. They said I'm ugly and have a big mouth."

My Mom looked at me like any Mom would and said, "Oh son, you're not ugly."

And then—silence.

She waited a beat or two and then continued, "But yes, you do have a big mouth. And you're just going to have to learn to live with that because that's how you came to this earth."

I was devastated. Even Mom thought I had a big mouth.

She then said, "You know, when people tell you to open your mouth or do that thing with your mouth, don't open it all big and wide like that; just smile!"

"Smile?" I asked.

"Yes! SMILE! Because the light you shine is the light you receive," she confidently proclaimed.

I didn't want to smile at everyone, as I was crying inside.

But she was right. Whenever someone came up and said, "Hey, do that thing with your mouth!" instead of opening it wide, I would instead SMILE.

And then they'd smile.

It was a miracle.

How grateful I am that my Mother taught me from such a young age that smiling at others usually results in them smiling back at you! *For the light we shine is the light we receive.*

*The light we shine is
the light we receive.*

Now, if you would, imagine with me this is you. This is your Mother telling you that you are okay, and even great, just the way you are. It's obviously helpful and a blessing to have someone say something like that.

This was the beginning of my own Self-Acceptance. To realize I had a Mom and Dad who saw value in me, that was a big deal. Not everyone has that. So where might it come from for others?

Perhaps you had a different situation than me. Hopefully your Self-Acceptance first came from friends, teachers, coaches, neighbors, community, or church leaders. Wherever the angels of your life arrived from, that is certainly a blessing.

But in reality, having these people tell us we are okay is one thing, yet it's never enough.

At some point, we need to realize it for ourselves, by ourselves, and not just rely on the acceptance others graciously toss our way; we need to find it in the recesses of our abilities, capabilities, and accomplishments.

And eventually in our values, that which makes up our moral compass.

As kids, and then as teenagers—even into adulthood—we often don't feel much Self-Acceptance.

This is because others win the school election, or get asked to prom by the one we hoped would ask us, or get the scholarship we were after, or the newspaper doesn't recognize us while everyone else seems to grab the headlines.

Then work becomes the space to hope for some kind of fulfillment, and we are passed over for the promotion even though it was us who did the most work, or we didn't get the raise, or we are the ones who struggle while everyone else seems to win the praise.

And then social media—oh social media! The Murderer of Self-Acceptance and great liar of false authenticity. And the cycle of discouragement and self-destructive thinking continues.

## SO WHERE IS THE PROMISE OF SELF-ACCEPTANCE?

Mine initially came from showing my big mouth to others and then realizing that the funny faces I could do, along with the vocal imitations I could do of everyone from the teacher to the kid sitting next to me, drew a laugh.

Getting laughs was my first feeling of Self-Acceptance.

And then I had a crisis: Are they laughing with me or at me?

For a while I didn't care. But then I really started to worry!

My Promise went from "Make them laugh no matter what" to "Make them laugh because it's extraordinary."

That made a huge difference in my life and shifted the standard for feeling Self-Acceptance.

Next crisis: Someone in the room was funnier than me. Uh-oh. Now what? Self-Acceptance gone?

Initially, yes, but then came another level of myself I didn't see coming: Authenticity and Vulnerability became my secret weapons.

While others perhaps could make someone laugh more than I could, I quickly discovered that I was capable of sharing authentically my own voice, thoughts, and cares. And I realized that this was another level of sharing.

I remember going to a new school. No friends. No one knew me.

I went for the thing that had made me popular at the last school: faces, voices, silliness.

New school: This did not go well.

So what would I do now? Am I out of "bits"? Am I worthless here and now?

No, I had other things I could go to, other offerings of who I am.

I became The Artist. I drew people in a caricature style, handed it to them, and they were stunned and then slowly became my friend. Quickly, I became known as The Art Guy.

And then eventually, they warmed to my faces, voices, and other talents, until finally I was known for those Signature Moves more than any others.

Another time and another school, when faces and funny weren't working because I wasn't the funniest one in the class, and when art didn't work as others were just as good, now it came time to be The Giver.

I gave compliments, not just to say something, but to truly honor the person and their efforts. I gave my time and volunteered for every opportunity to serve. This has become one of the greatest habits of my life. To be The Giver became my Signature Move in the eyes of many people.

My peers and teachers knew that if something had to be done, if anyone would volunteer, it would be me. First one to pick up trash in the hall, first to say "hello" to the new guy, first to encourage participation in class when I noticed the teacher was struggling.

Eventually I even did this Giver concept for the teachers by way of putting my hand up to be the one to do the hardest tasks, help students in need, even to compliment their efforts when the class got out of hand...and they were shocked, as no student ever did this type of thing without a hidden agenda.

I still run into teachers from three decades ago who remind me of this behavior, and they always say, "School wasn't easy for you, but we all knew you were going to do something extraordinary with your life."

The Funny Guy • The Artist • The Giver

Does this resonate with you?

All I am saying is this is The Promise. The exploration and identification of Self, of all you have to offer—even if it's not the most extraordinary gift, like just being The Giver, which any person can do—can elevate you to new levels of living, leadership, and loving your unique Self.

This is The Promise of Self-Acceptance: to continually allow others to feel the goodness that is you, which equates to self-confidence in your ability to contribute, to make a difference, to be the reliable helper when others are in need.

The problem with Self-Acceptance is that so often we come at the world with our one talent—our Signature Moves, as it were—and realize quickly that we aren't the only one with that skill or gift, just as I did when trying to be The Funny Guy and realizing that wasn't hitting the mark.

And then literally, we stop using it! That Signature Move was pretty much our one giant cannon to break down the wall, and when it doesn't make a dent we quickly retreat into the recesses of the forest, only to hide all our other gifts forever.

This is truly the worst thing one can do.

Think of yourself going after the girl of your dreams, knowing she is the one and you have no shot. I have been there, and I have done that. There was literally NO WAY I was going to get the girl of my dreams.

My first major rejection came in high school when I saw a girl that so knocked me out I did everything to get her attention—from being the funny guy, to making noises and voices, to frightening her away.

When I saw she liked athletes, what did I do? I became The Athlete! I worked all summer to become better with that desire in mind to make the team and win her over.

The drive to succeed because of love is a powerful thing, and for me I was in love! So I did what it took.

I returned the next year, went from last guy on the bench of the JV basketball team to being the starter on the varsity team. It was an unprecedented leap! And yet, did it win her over? No!

I noticed she gave compliments to a friend of ours who drew portraits, not just funny pictures and cartoons. So I began to draw portraits! I drew a picture of her that was incredible. It took me the entire summer. I'll never forget handing it to her the next fall, and she barely gave it a look or a chance. I was floored! I was torn apart!

When drawing didn't work, I realized she loved music, and that's when I discovered I could sing! Now I became The Singer! I began singing and working on my talent with the gusto of an artist who's realized he's had an unreleased treasure that was now the soaring gem of his life. My voice!

And so I sang. To her. She swooned and smiled—and then ended up in the arms of another guy!

Devastated, I wondered, *How do I win this girl?*

And then I stepped back and realized what had just happened. In my pursuit of this mythic creature and unicorn of our school, I had gone from silly and bizarre in my humor to sophisticated and pretty brilliant in my ability to make people laugh, I had become the top three-point shooter in the state and won All-State honors in basketball, and I had gone from wannabe artist to discovering a whole different level of ability in my artistry as The Singer!

In working to win over a girl who would never be mine, I had developed talents that have gone on to define my entire life! But it's because I didn't stop working to find new ways to impress, receive acknowledgment, and discover more of myself.

All of this practice, these invaluable gifts, still serve me to this day. She was a real angel in my life. Even though she never saw anything in me that resembled attraction, she drove me to my own Self-Acceptance and confidence in making Promises to myself to become great at any skill I devoted myself to learning.

Whatever your reason or method may be, think of how you came to be who and what you are now, at this point in your life.

Because I never won that girl, it taught me a few valuable lessons, one of which is that you can only do so much to win the approval of others, even when you have world-class talent that they don't recognize.

This became a refiner's fire moment for me. Self-assurance I had, due to hours and hours, days and weeks, of practice. For me, it was assurance in my relentless pursuit of practicing skills I didn't know would benefit me throughout my life but now make up the entirety of it.

And then, guess what happened? After years of refinement, of honing my talents and skills, of sharing my comedy, faces, voices, and art, of hard work and dedication to becoming a better person, instead of winning over the girl I wanted as part of a pipe dream, I became the type of man that a woman would want to be with. And then it happened.

She appeared.

The actual Girl of My Dreams.

And I married her.

Ugly, old, big-mouthed, weird kid, me.

She said "Yes."

It's a miracle, really.

And if you know my wife, you know I'm the Winner. She did alright, but I'm the Winner.

Her accepting and choosing me is simply a result of my never giving up on me. Because really, it's impossible that she chose me.

Yes, I still hunted her down, and I did all it took to win her over, but I call it a Win.

The biggest WIN of my life.

Self-Assurance, Self-Acceptance, never stopping, never quitting—that is your Promise.

If you come at life with one skill, one gift, and you think that's enough, pretty much it never will be.

## SO WHAT ARE YOU WAITING FOR?

Are you waiting for life to hand you the prize? Do you need to win something in order to be accepting of yourself?

When you make a Promise to yourself and then you keep it, that is the greatest feeling in the world.

Think of those nights you go to sleep motivated to wake up early, set your alarm, and dream of waking up and going for that jog.

And then the alarm goes off at 5:00 A.M. You usually wake up at 7:00 A.M., but not today—today it's 5:00 A.M. and you are going to conquer this day!

You JUMP out of bed, put on those shoes, and sprint out the door.

You have kept a Promise to yourself. You feel incredible. That is The Promise of Self-Acceptance. That is having faith in yourself to do what you said you'd do, an inner strength and drive that few accomplishments in life can match.

No recognition from others, no acceptance from a peer, boss, or spouse, can fill the void in the same way as when you keep a Promise to yourself and actually follow through with it.

When your coach moves on, when you change grades and have a new teacher, when you shift jobs and have a new manager and suddenly they are moved to another department, when your child grows up and stops looking at you like their hero and instead sees you as their enemy, and if your spouse were to pass tragically before their time, you have to be able to draw on your own reserves. Anything in life can happen that can destroy your hopes, dreams, and the validation that others bring.

But if you have made a Promise to yourself to say what you're going to do, and then you do it, no matter what happens to you in life with relationships, disappointment, and even the loss of freedom and ability, if you can wake up and keep The Promise that you made the night before, that is the essence of Self-Acceptance.

Nothing is sweeter. Nothing is more powerful. Some may call it faith in itself; others, the will to continue, but your language from this day forward becomes:

"I made myself a Promise. I never break a Promise to myself. Get up. Now."

Promise kept.

## EXERCISE: SELF-ACCEPTANCE

Write an entire page in your journal forgiving yourself of the mean things you've said about yourself.

Write on the other side of the page how you Promise to treat and talk to yourself from now on.

# CHAPTER 5

# HABITS

---

*It is easy to make promises—
it is hard work to keep them.*

—BORIS JOHNSON

Greatness is a Habit. Success is a Habit. You've heard this all before. Let's try a new one:

## PROMISES ARE HABITS.

Our lives are made up of kept or broken Promises.

This behavior becomes our Habit pattern and eventually the Rituals that rule our lives.

Generally, I sleep on the same side of the bed each night, check my phone and plug it in the same place, have the habit of misplacing my keys and glasses, and scramble through my e-mails to file them away in order to have my inbox at zero, only to realize I've simply filed away everything that needs to be done.

I wake up pretty much at the same time every day and am awakened nightly by the aging process that forces me to visit the bathroom twice per night (that and the Habit of drinking a 48-ounce glass of water before bed, which I've done my whole life). I bite my nails, brush my teeth more than morning and night, and can't stop tugging on my collar to get it to stay up whenever I wear a suit without a tie.

You have yours, I have mine, and our Habits make up the lives we lead.

What do Habits have to do with Promises?

I can easily change my Habit if I make a new Promise.

## A PROMISE IS THE ACTIVE AGENT OF SHIFTING PERMANENT BEHAVIOR.

If I consciously decide not to get up in the middle of the night, such as when I go camping and really don't want to be disturbed if by chance I fall asleep, I make sure not to drink any water after 7:00 P.M. I make a very little, easy Promise that I won't have a sip of water, no matter how much my body begs for it, in order to fall asleep and stay asleep.

Promises make up our daily lives, because Habits dictate our rituals, which guide our moment-to-moment existence.

If I have created the Habit of checking my phone every time I am bored or there's a stop in the action, then I have made a Promise not to be present and fully engaged in the moment.

If I get in my car, seat belt on, radio tuned in to my favorite station, seat in the perfect spot, then I am ready for my ride. But if my wife has used my car, everything is a complete mess: my seat refuses to find its perfect place again, my radio is on some channel I'd never choose to listen to, and certainly that rearview mirror will take weeks to find its way back to normal.

Our response to the disruption of our Habits by others or circumstances, and our infusion of them into the way we choose to proceed through life, is a Promise to keep our lives the way we feel is most comfortable.

Habits are our neutral setting. Promises become the same thing.

And so, if I stop at a red light and have to wait for more than five seconds, naturally I have created the Habit of grabbing my phone to check messages and see what's going on.

In most parts of the world, at this point I am doing something illegal that wasn't deemed against the law when I first created the Habit.

If I want to remain a good citizen and not be the one sitting there holding up traffic once the light turns green because I'm sucked into some Facebook drama on my neighborhood group page, then I need to make a new Habit—and that comes in making a new Promise.

Perhaps I need to delete the app? Maybe I should put the phone in my pocket? What is my solution for changing the pattern?

My Promise now becomes an active agreement with myself: When I am behind the wheel, no matter if I am stopped or driving, I am fully focused and not looking at my phone.

For some people reading this, my dilemma may sound atrocious. You're thinking, "What kind of sick individual is this?" Hey, you have Habits I don't love either, so just realize what we are discussing here.

The shifting of one's Habits either comes at the peril of a life-changing accident or the realization that behavior must change! Either the diagnosis that yes, you need to stop eating sugar or smoking or you will literally die, or the foresight and self-awareness to recognize that yes, your Habit must change.

## TAKE INVENTORY—

When was the last time you considered your Habits? Are they building you up or destroying you?

If you would like a fast track to finding out how your Habits are affecting your life and loved ones, go ahead and ask them. Do your best not to start screaming when they tell you the truth.

These are your Habits, for heck's sake! They are what you not only created, but what you've become, and they are the most comfortable, comforting things that you do without thought. Careful what anyone says!

Since you are reading this book, you have a desire to live at a different level. Those are the only people still reading at this point. I welcome you to the "What Have I Gotten Myself Into?" section of The Promise.

# EXERCISE: HABITS

Stop reading for one whole minute and notice what you do with your body.

Okay, go—I mean it, stop! Stop reading and notice. Go!

What did you notice?

Maybe you're nothing like me, but I noticed some very small things that would probably drive someone bonkers if they were sitting in this room with me, such as...the second I stopped reading, I:

- cracked my knuckles

- blinked and moved my glasses around my face without using my hands (because I was cracking my knuckles)

- scrunched up my toes and rubbed my socks together to make a hideous sound

- grabbed my cup full of ice water and chomped loudly with my mouth open

- bit my pinky fingernail, which hardly remains

- checked my phone

- and looked at my timer to see, aghast, only 25 seconds had passed!

I admit, I have ticks and little things I do that completely annoy the heck out of people around me and even bug me that I do them.

How do I stop them?

Conscious Creation of my Promises.

Whatever my intention is, from now on I will work on those Habits.

For example, for years I have been off and on with biting my nails—really not a great Habit for sure. How can I resist? I mean, between that and smoking, the smoker has a way easier time quitting.

"No way!" you protest?

Okay, let's examine.

The smoker has to pull a cigarette out of their pocket, have a lighter, and go to a place in the location where smoking is allowed or acceptable. If the smoker doesn't have a cigarette, they have to get up, put clothes on, find car keys, drive to the store, show their ID, purchase the cigarettes, and then go find somewhere without wind to light up and smoke his Habit.

Compare this to the nail biter.

The nail biter simply has to look at his hands and the nail comes at him like a wave of never-ending opportunity. It is the equivalent of cigarettes growing out of the ends of your fingers!

So let's be honest here—all Habits have the same power over us, no matter how great or small.

When I go to bite my nails, I do that without thinking. So now it's a matter of thinking consciously this very thought—one word:

Nope.

That's it. That's my Promise not to bite my nails.

That sounds so easy, and yet it's so profoundly difficult.

Now think of your Habit, whether it's overeating, sleeping in, binge-watching Netflix all night, listening to talk radio on your commute home instead of an edifying audiobook.

Consider your Habits in business, with e-mails, phone calls, texts, which tasks you do first, calendar items, and conference calls, meetings and where you sit...you name it, you are a creature of Habit!

## *Change the Habit if it's not serving you.*

Change the Habit if it's not serving you.

Make a NEW Promise.

My Promise word is simple: *Nope.*

If I reach for that donut sitting on the counter staring at me, seducing me with its custard and frosting outfit, all I say is, "Nope."

If a client tells me they need more information than is available on my website or require a complete run-through of my presentation line by line, bit by bit, to approve my every word, my initial thought, reaction, and Habit is to tell them to go jump in a lake. But then I stop and say, "Nope. I will do what they asked since they are my client."

If my child receives a C or below on their report card, my initial Habit is to start in on a lecture about getting good grades, but instead I say, "Nope. Calm down. Let's ask what's going on here..."

That's my Promise to Self. And it literally affects everyone around me at all times when I am willing to be conscious of my Habits.

Sipping my cup of ice water alone in my office and loudly chewing my ice, mouth wide open, shards of frozen water flying from my face...that's fine, as long as no one is around.

I didn't realize how disturbing my ice chewing really is until I was sitting in a movie theater with my son and the person next to me was glaring at me as I happily sipped my drink and chewed my ice. I truly had no idea why they were upset. I said, "What?" He said, "Why are you chewing ice loud enough for everyone to hear?"

Ouch!

Point taken.

I didn't even realize I did it!

So, take inventory of your Habits, and come up with your word or phrase that will help you right the behavior you don't even realize you're doing.

My word, remember, is, "Nope." What's yours going to be?

What's funny is that you will find yourself saying the word out loud even when no one is around. I'm sure housekeepers in hotels around the world are gearing up for a real loud knock to come clean my room when they hear a loud, "Nope!" from behind my door as I close the mini fridge and deny the $17 M&M's box from ruining my sugar-free living.

When I've asked my family, they've told me they don't like the way I do certain things, such as filming us doing family activities, trying to say funny things to their friends, and playing the piano too loudly when they're watching TV.

Asking family, co-workers, and friends which of our Habits bother them can hurt your ego, but there is no better way to make a new Habit and keep your Promise than to accept what you've become and begin to shift behavior from destructive to constructive.

## EXERCISE 2: HABITS

Stop reading once again, but this time, instead of focusing on your body and the Habits you naturally do, now just focus on what the voice in your head is telling you.

Listen to that voice. Go.

Okay.

If you're like me, you went to the easiest place in your mind possible:

You went to your to-do list!

We do this because we figure that sitting quietly is a waste of time, and so when we're done thinking and listening to our inner voice we are not going to waste any more time!

Are you with me?

All the inner voice is doing is stepping on your subconscious voice, because that's the one that usually wins. It's louder as the voice of drive and accomplishment; it's the fight-or-flight mechanism.

The subconscious voice is nearly impossible to make out under all the noise of your to-do list.

Silence is now the key and the most important part of your improvement.

Tapping into your subconscious allows you to alter your behavior and go after those Habits.

Your subconscious doesn't need to think to act; it just does what it's programmed to do. So reprogram it. But you need space for silence. Chop through the noise. Find the quiet and peace and calm.

Now, when you subconsciously do one of your Habits, do the following:

1. STOP and recognize the Habit!

2. Acknowledge that it's there and real and something you do every time.

3. Determine for yourself, or ask a trusted friend, if it builds you up or is self-destructive.

4. If you realize it's destructive, establish your Promise word when it manifests.

5. If you realize it builds you up, establish your Promise word to continue the behavior.

When I realize a Habit is a good one, such as sticking to my plan, keeping my commitment, and becoming the best person I can be, I say my other Promise word:

Yes!

I may even do a little Kip Dynamite fist pump and do his voice in my head: "Yesssss!"

Shaping your subconscious actions is the essence of The Promise.

In this way, you no longer have to think about actively making Promises in every place in your life; rather, it becomes a Habit. Your Habits are the summation of your output to the world.

*Your Habits are the summation of your output to the world.*

Not happy with where you are in life, love, success, and feel the whole world is against you?

Consider your Habits, your patterns, the Rituals that make up your existence. Inner peace comes from knowing you are keeping The Promise of manifesting Habits that result in creation rather than destruction, which spills over into every aspect of your existence.

Embrace the silence. Listen to your subconscious. Face your Habits, and make new Promises.

What you don't like about yourself you have created. Change your Habits, and change your life.

That's The Promise.

# CHAPTER 6

# KINDNESS

---

*People with good intentions make promises
but people with good character keep them.*

—ANONYMOUS

Our young basketball team was killing the other team. There is nothing more fun than winning—and winning easily—and knowing your team is superior and you've chosen the right guys to go to battle with.

In business, this is a good feeling. As The Leader, you know you are surrounded with talent, go-getters, and winners. Go for it. Kill the competition. That is certainly a huge part of The Promise—that when you're up in war, battle, or competition, you strike.

And then there's the youth basketball league, filled with kids learning the game. Everyone gets equal time to play because this isn't a "comp" league; it's rec ball, and everyone is there to have fun, learn, and decide whether this is a sport worth pursuing.

My son had asked me to coach his basketball team, so as I watched the advantage my team had, with my son's best friends and the other players we had chosen to give us the upper hand, I realized there is a very important aspect to The Promise in this instance of winning.

I looked at the terrified boys on the other team, then observed the frustration on the opposing coach's face. Across the court I could see the concern of parents and grandparents who were there to support their kids too.

Timeout.

Huddled together, our team was so happy. This was the first game, and we were killing them. I too was excited, seeing smiles and laughs from our team's parents as well, and of course I didn't want to lessen their thrill.

But we needed to keep this enjoyable for the other team as well.

I asked the boys, ages 10 and 11, in the huddle, "Guys, you're doing amazing. We have such a talented, tall, and tough team. It's great! Question: Have you noticed how much more you understand the game, and how much better you play, than the other team?"

"Yes!" they exclaimed, "Their team stinks! They don't even know how to dribble or shoot, and we are stealing every pass and blocking every shot!"

"Yes," I said, "And if we were playing a team like you guys, how would you feel being on the other end of this?"

They looked confused.

I said, "Guys, look, we are probably going to win every game we play this season. That is awesome. I want you to play your best and always go for the win. I also want you all to learn every aspect of the game so you can play every position and become better players and people. At the same time, we want the other team to have a great experience as well. How can we do that without just handing them the ball?"

One by one these young men piped in:

"Maybe we could play zone defense instead of man-to-man and not go for the steal every single time..."

"What if we guard them but with our hands down, instead of up, and when they shoot we don't go for the block, but only when they come in the paint..."

"How about we celebrate when we score, but also congratulate them when they do?"

These were the types of solutions I was hoping they'd come up with. These are the kinds of boys you want on your team. I assured them they could still steal the ball when a weak pass was made but directed them not to steal it from a kid learning to dribble; that they could still block the shot, just not outside the key. They understood.

It wasn't with the intention of rolling over and handing the other team the ball. We didn't want our guys to slow down, to shoot with their left hand if they were right-handed. I wasn't telling them to wrap a bandana around their head to play with one eye closed. Rather, we wanted to give everyone a chance to have a good experience on both sides.

With a comfortable lead, I sent them back out on the floor and made the center play point guard, and moved the point guard to center, shooting guards to forward, and vice versa—balanced the chances out across the game in little ways that allowed our players to improve on their weaknesses in ways they hadn't explored when focusing only on their strengths.

I told them they needed to do four passes before they could shoot, and other times that our only goal was to give a certain kid who didn't score the whole game the green light to shoot, and that no one else was allowed to shoot until he did. This forged a togetherness and helpfulness in our young team.

They saw that Kindness is a virtue that is worth cultivating, even when playing a competitive game.

How can we involve everyone and make each player on our team, as well as on the other team, feel like they are a part of the game?

I went to the teenage referees and asked, "Hey guys, you're calling a good game, but if you see my team get the ball and shuffle their feet, I need you to call a travel. Call 'travel' on my guys religiously. Do not miss a travel on our team. Do whatever you need to do with calls for the other team, but no matter what, do not miss a travel, foul, or double dribble with my players. Do you understand?"

They looked at me completely dumbfounded. "You want us to call 'travel' on your team?"

"Yes, IF they travel! Don't just call a travel—call it if they do it. You've missed a bunch of them from my players, and I need them to learn that they need to stop shuffling their feet when they get the ball. We worked on it in practice, but if you don't call it during the game they'll never improve," I demanded.

A big smile came across their faces as they realized what I was doing. One leaned in and said, "No coach has ever told us to call something on their own team. You're like a real coach."

I patted him on the back and said, "And you're a real referee, doing a good job. Go call 'travel' when you see it from my guys."

Quickly, all of these little changes shifted the game. My team wasn't getting away with those little issues we couldn't fix in practice because the refs were on it! The center playing point guard had to quickly learn how to protect his dribble and the point guard had to learn to guard a guy bigger than him.

Suddenly, the other team even caught the ball and dribbled, almost making a shot! Our team cheered for his attempt and almost missed the rebound. I could see parents of the opposing team turn from despair to hope and the coach go from despondent and feeling like a failure to realizing they had a shot.

Down the court our team went, set up, and easily scored. High fives all around. It was great.

Next time down the court the other team actually scored. The entire gym went bonkers, and our team cheered for them. I even noticed my players' parents were in on it just by osmosis, and they began clapping for anything good by both teams.

I shuffled my players to positions with which they weren't comfortable but that pushed their abilities to new levels. We did all kinds of variations on defense and offense to equalize the opportunity, and even though we won every game but two very easily that season, it proved the point that needed to be made:

## KINDNESS WINS.

Kindness is The Promise.

Kindness doesn't mean weakness and being pathetic. Often men—manly men—especially in sports, forget sportsmanship and choose a different reaction.

If you're being paid to compete and it's your livelihood, or you're in a competitive league and winning is the name of the game, then be kind before the game and after the game. No need to equalize the playing field. Go for the win.

Greet the other players with respect, and play your heart out for the prize, and always shake hands afterward.

But at the same time, remember, we are all still human beings. It is sad to watch sports that celebrate gloating, chest thumping, and guys dunking on someone and then stepping over them when they're down. I know coaches who will pull the player off the court for showing that kind of disrespect to another human being.

Kindness can still exist in competition, be it helping an opposing player up off the floor, running to their side if they're injured, or holding your teammates back in a heated scuffle.

One of the most magnificent displays of Kindness I've ever seen was by the NBA's strongest player, Steven Adams of the Oklahoma City Thunder, as he went up for a shot. He faked it, and the defender jumped so high that when Adams went back up to shoot, the defender was now falling headfirst toward the ground over the top of Adams's body without his hands available to stop his inevitable fall.

In that instant, 99.9 percent of players in any sport would take advantage of the opening and easily score, while the other player tumbles past or over them and is perhaps permanently injured.

Not Steven Adams.

Somehow, in that split second, he realized this defender was going to land on his head and probably seriously injure himself, maybe even break his neck and ruin his life.

In a millionth of a second, Adams showed the kind of character he has as a man, who made a subconscious Promise at some point in his life that someone's well-being, whether on his team or the opposing one, is more important than him scoring a minor two points.

He dropped the ball and used his hands and arms, as the strongest man in the league, to catch this opponent against his own body before the defender's head hit the ground.

It was one of the greatest displays of Kindness I've ever witnessed at a sporting event, and should be the thought process of every athlete, competitor, salesperson, or business leader.

The basket wasn't made, the points weren't gained, but the respect of the entire sports world for Adams in this moment became his Signature Move and Promise—that he cared more for the well-being of an opponent than an easy basket.

The player was set on the ground, he was fine, and the game went on. But I'll never forget that moment—a split-second reaction that, in all reality, was a decision made long before that play.

Adams must have been raised to be a kind person—and yes, still a strong, buff, tough dude, but a kind and respectful person first.

So, if you're a competitor and going for the win where your paycheck and your living are on the line, then go for it, unless of course someone's well-being is at stake.

But if you're coaching kids' sports, and everyone is learning all around you how to survive a simple catch and shoot moment, try this: Be kind.

Kindness stems from attentiveness. Open your eyes. Look up from your phone. Take out your earbuds and hear what's going on all around you.

## KINDNESS BREEDS KARMA.

Upgraded from coach to first class on my flight to Atlanta, I sat in my big, comfy, roomy seat. Stuffing my pillow and blankie in the seat pocket, comforts that only first-class passengers get, I settled in for the long flight.

The woman seated beside me suddenly handed her special pillow to the man passing us, as her husband walked by and sat behind us.

In coach.

I asked, "Is that your husband?"

"Yes," she responded.

Getting up out of my seat, I walked to him and asked, "Sir, do you mind if we trade seats so you can sit with your lovely bride?"

"Yes?" he said, confused. "Are you sure?" he asked.

"Of course!" I replied. "I was upgraded, so essentially I lose nothing, and I'm happy that you get to sit with your wife, as I'd love to sit with mine if she were on this trip with me."

You would have thought I handed him a $1,000 check.

Grateful and shocked, he got up and took his seat next to his wife in first class, while I took my seat happily in coach.

He looked back and said, "Thank you so much. That was so very thoughtful of you."

The truth is, yes, that was thoughtful, but I'm sure plenty of people would have had a similar thought and yet probably do nothing about it. And perhaps even more people would have never had the thought to begin with because they're so zoned into their phone and not noticing the many ways we can be kind to those around us all the time.

Opportunities abound for Kindness and keeping a Promise, whether you realized you made the Promise to be kind or not.

This isn't to say, "Yay for me!" as I believe there are others out there who would do the same given the circumstance, but the question is, how often do we take advantage of our chance to be kind, to serve others, when we notice the opportunity?

Especially nowadays.

We just need to keep our eyes open and our hearts in that place that allows us to give where we can.

Make a new friend, even a stranger on a plane, and take care of each other.

There's actually a funny twist to the story...

Before the plane took off, the man who took my place in first class was suddenly upgraded to first class anyway!

So, he gave me his seat!

We laughed and are now friends. Funny how things work out.

But my sitting in first class doesn't make me automatically a first-class person; that is the kind of person I strive to be no matter where I find myself.

If you realize you are living a life of Kindness, then I applaud you for it. If you are reading these stories and not relating in any way to what has been shared, if there is a complete disconnect to what I'm saying, then try this—

## EXERCISE: KINDNESS

Scroll through your Contacts on your phone.

Pick a friend, any friend, whom you haven't texted or called in a while.

Think of a few nice things about them and either call and tell them or text it to them.

If they respond by asking, "Are you dying or something?" then yes, you need to share more Kindness—and more often.

Make Kindness a daily practice. One of the best ways I know to do this is to make a concerted effort to support and uplift the efforts of my peers on social media. Instead of just mindlessly scrolling through my feed, I notice every post and give some encouragement in a like and comment.

This may sound very simple and almost too easy. But try it.

The next level is to see what people in your feed are selling. And then buy it!

Okay, maybe not everyone wants to buy the latest MLM pitch. But I always buy the book or online learning program, or support the fundraiser and charity, about which my friends are talking.

If I like the book or product, then I will take a photo of myself and share it to my network.

This is Kindness. This is active effort in making someone's day, with no thought or expectation of them returning the favor... which they often don't. And that's fine.

This is The Promise.

How often are you doing the same for others?

If it's too awkward to start by communicating with a distant contact via text, e-mail, phone call, or social media, then try it with a loved one, a child who feels disconnected. What is their favorite thing to do? Play video games? Ask to play with them.

## KINDNESS IS CONNECTION.

As you self-assess, record in your journal some of the impressions you have about expressing and becoming a kinder person. I don't recall the last time I made an active effort to be extra kind that I didn't come away feeling like it was the best thing I could do with that time.

Kindness fills the soul, establishes purpose, and makes the day of another.

Now let's close this portion with Kindness to You.

How kind are you to yourself? When you look in the mirror, are you mean to the incredible, amazing, beautiful, and magnificent person staring back at you?

I'm not going to get all oogly here and tell you to go Richard Smalley and do a bunch of affirmations, although you're free to do as you feel—"Coz gosh darnit, I like myself!"

Instead, maybe you're like me and you have a hard time even looking in the mirror and liking anything about yourself.

Yes, I feel that way, if we can be candid here.

So this is what I do. I look at myself. I see the flaws, the cheat meals that make up my love handles, the fingernails that are bitten too low, the eyes deprived of sleep...and I bow my head, and instead of judging myself too harshly I simply....

Say a Prayer of Gratitude.

Gratitude for life. That I have a body in the first place. That I have hands that work, that I have eyes that see. My body's nowhere near the physical shape I want it to be in, and oftentimes my mind isn't where you would imagine it ought to be.

But I'm grateful for life. I'm grateful for this day. I'm grateful for every waking moment.

And then I resolve to Promise to be kind. Be kind to myself. Not beat myself up for where I'm lacking, not kick myself for my failed efforts or stupid mistakes, and not judge myself.

I forgive myself a lot. Pretty much all day. I journal a lot! I write a lot! And I express my gratitude to others for the gift they are to me.

If you are having a hard time being kind to yourself, go express Gratitude to others for what they have done—in your life, relationships, career, or for your heart.

And then express Gratitude to God for your life and your health, no matter what condition you're in, no matter your situation, no matter how strapped your finances may be.

And then, be kind to yourself.

I've noticed when I travel that I won't eat for hours on end. I won't go out of my way to help myself out. And I suffer.

Yet if I travel with a loved one, I buy extravagant things—the best meals, the greatest gifts. I won't buy myself nice headphones, but I will buy them for those that refer me for events.

Why do we do this? Why aren't we kind to ourselves?

For me it's a constant reminder that I should be kind to myself.

And I remind myself of this again, and again, and again.

That's when I get up and go for a walk in whatever city I may find myself in while speaking and traveling. That's when I get my workout in, treat myself to a nice meal, and buy myself that special something that I would be willing to buy for someone else and that I want for me.

Kindness is Practice. Kindness is Patience. Kindness is perhaps harder for you to show yourself than anyone else.

Kindness is a Top Priority.

That's The Promise.

# CHAPTER 7

# SERVICE

---

*One promises much, to avoid giving little.*

—LUC DE CLAPIERS

In suburbia there is a phenomenon that occurs with each and every season. I call it "Property Line Living."

When it snows in the winter, I look outside after 9:00 A.M. and can see who's on my team and who's not. One neighbor usually has shoveled his driveway, walkway, and steps, and then there's the sidewalk...which is shoveled exactly to my property line.

I glance over at the other neighbor's home and see the snow piling up.

I know both neighbors have kids capable of doing the shoveling. Both are able-bodied families that can do whatever they want with their property and their snow!

Yet I have found it fascinating what happens each time I'm the first one out to shovel, before any neighbors, as to the feeling I experience inside.

It is a battle within.

Usually, I am in a hurry to get my driveway, walkway, steps, and sidewalk portion cleared. If I stop at the property lines, I feel physically sick about it. I feel I have somehow let my neighbors and community down. Those days, when my schedule calls or I'm late for a flight, I rush off, having done only my property.

And then there are the days when no one knows my schedule, whether I have a flight out or not, when I could easily take as much time as I want to just do my own property's snow removal or help the neighbors out a little.

If I have the time and there is nothing else to rush off to—I'm still not sure when, where, or why I made this Promise—but I shovel beyond the property lines.

After clearing my own snow-covered responsibilities, I work my way to one neighbor or the other's sidewalk portion. Eventually, I clear their smaller driveways and steps. Rarely have I been caught in this act of service, and only once that I recall in 10 years has either of them said anything publicly about it.

The magic snow removal fairy is a simple Promise, but a Promise indeed.

It's more for my own peace of mind and sense of community than anything else.

The concept and perception that we are in Property Line Living country doesn't resonate with my spirit, so I make it a point to smash that whole notion to bits and create my own version of being a neighbor.

When I am shoveling, especially during the winters we've had of late, I feel complete joy and gratitude about the water that must be filling the reservoirs in our mountains, the snow falling that will attract visitors to our state, and the exercise it is for my body. To be outdoors, to enjoy a nice audiobook, classical music, a TED Talk, or my religious leaders speak in conference—this fills my soul.

Service is a major part of The Promise and should be a top priority in your living The Promise lifestyle.

Whether it's shoveling your neighbors' snow in the dead of winter, raking their leaves in the fall, or sweeping the water away as spring makes its way to the gutters, there is service all around us that needs not be divided by property lines.

The world is divided in its view of others. So often we stand in our place, seeing suffering on the news or challenges others face, and we feel that we can only do so much. So instead of sending a check to the orphans who are starving, we turn the channel to escape our sadness and find a place to laugh.

I am guilty of this—and even have served as the person to create the escape and laughter!

I am grateful to have this gift of making others smile and forget their worries, and at the same time I feel the responsibility to serve whenever and wherever possible, as much as I can.

Perhaps this is why the property lines division and connection resonates to such an extent for me.

If I can't change the world over there, at least I can serve the world right here.

*If I can't change the world*
*over there, at least I can serve*
*the world right here.*

## THE PROMISE OF SERVICE IS ACTIVE HELPFULNESS.

It is getting involved, lifting the downtrodden, and even giving to those who aren't in need, such as my neighbors, just because serving lifts your own spirit and brings you joy.

The question is: Do you find ways to serve, and if so, how often?

If Service isn't a Habit in your Promise lifestyle, then what are you doing with your life?

I have never served another and thought, "Well, that was a waste of time."

I've certainly felt, "Well, they didn't appreciate that!" or "I'm sure they could have done that themselves!" But I do the service mostly because I Promise to Serve.

In your business, you may not get asked to do your work for free. If you are an entrepreneur, then maybe you've been asked to donate to a cause, or if you own a restaurant you've had kids come by doing fundraising looking for a handout.

But this request for Service takes on a whole new level for the "Entertainer" or "Speaker" whose time seems to be worth tens of thousands per hour to some and next to nothing to most.

I receive in my inbox a daily average of three requests for my time, expertise, and donation to causes, charitable and not. Each one is weighed differently. If I said "yes" to all of them, I would have been out of business before I began nearly 20 years ago, but we do our best to give where possible.

Often the request to do favors for a friend comes up, family occasionally, religious and education groups mostly, but there is one for which I dropped everything—and how grateful I am that I chose to do so!

In July 2014, I flew to Afghanistan to perform for the front-line soldiers fighting the war against terrorism in our U.S. Troops and Allies. It was the trip of a lifetime. In nearly a month-long tour, performing in everywhere from grand halls to makeshift tents, from hospitals to lunch rooms and kitchens, we seemed to do multiple shows per day in order to lift the spirits of those who needed a little taste of home.

To have men come up to you in full uniform, in camo, carrying assault rifles, with tears in their eyes, saying, "Thank you. You're my hero for coming to lift our spirits," well, this was about as humbling of an experience as one can have.

When heroes call you a hero, it's pretty apparent they needed your service.

They claimed they asked others more famous, and because of the danger of the situation, the celebrity acts had turned down the opportunity to serve their country in that time of need for those people serving us. Apparently I was the only one willing to go, along with my travel group of speakers and performers.

*When heroes call you a hero, it's pretty apparent they needed your service.*

My career began in my early 20s, and I never made the decision to serve our country, but I made a Promise to my wife that if they ever came calling I would go wherever they needed me!

That's an easy Promise to make when you don't have kids and are a newlywed.

Fast-forward 13 years, we had four kids under the age of 10, and we get the call to serve...in the deadliest war zone in the world. I called my wife and told her this was the greatest way we as a family could serve our country. Thankfully, she agreed.

I upgraded my life insurance policy, wrote letters to the kids, and wrapped presents for every birthday I would miss in their young lives if I were to perish, and soon I was flying across the world to inspire the troops.

There were moments that were terrifying, such as when we flew over a spot in the mountains of Afghanistan and the pilot pointed out the region where the Taliban was always doing target practice. Suddenly, we heard the sound of rounds hitting our

Chinook! Returning fire with machine guns, we went into a drop pattern that helped us avoid being shot down.

Seated next to Hall of Fame speaker Dan Clark, who had organized the trip, we looked at each other in terror, while across the way I saw world-famous musician and voice teacher Dean Kaelin hanging on for dear life as we all yelled for American Idol finalist David Archuleta to put on his helmet!

Upon landing, we were quite shaken, but we performed anyway. We were thankful to be alive. Our Promise to serve had brought us here, to those that serve as their Promise to the world.

It was a humbling experience, that entire trip, and it changed my perspective on caring for those over whom we have stewardship.

Most of us will never know the life of those in the military, the sacrifice and struggles they face, but we all know someone who is family of military, and their sacrifice is often even greater by being the one who is left home. Ask a soldier—they'll tell you the same. They would ask you to serve their families before worrying about the soldier.

Property Line Living makes up the majority of our lives, and Service is The Promise to connect any division.

*Property Line Living makes up the majority of our lives, and Service is The Promise to connect any division.*

When we wonder whom can we serve and what we can do to be of Service to those in need, just look around. Ask a friend or neighbor, join a community outreach, or serve in your church.

If you feel unable to serve, just remember—Service is everywhere; you simply have to keep your eyes and ears open.

My wife and I were at the store late one night after a long day at Disneyland. Suddenly, we heard screams and ran to see what was happening.

A man was on the ground, kneeling over a small child, who apparently had just suffered a seizure. Yelling and crying in Spanish, the man was pleading for help.

Store employees ran to help but weren't trained as to what to do. My wife called 911 as a majority of the forming crowd stood by and watched, helpless and unhelpful.

Finally, a person came running up, grabbed the boy, and checked his vitals, as he wasn't moving and didn't appear to be breathing. The Dad was kneeling down, sobbing, not sure if his little child was going to make it.

I looked around to see if I could do anything to help. I felt helpless.

And then I heard cries. Small voice cries.

Looking through the crowd of people I saw a grocery cart, with a car seat in a box to be purchased, and two little girls huddled next to it, crying and hugging one another.

I went over and knelt down behind them as they cried. I asked, "Is that your baby brother?" The older of the little girls nodded yes. I asked, "Do you speak English?" She said, "Yes." I asked,

"Where's your Mommy?" She said, "She is at the hospital. She just had a baby today, and our Dad was buying a new car seat, and then our brother started shaking and fell over. Is he going to die?"

I said, "No, he will be fine, but let's say a prayer." As I knelt with these two little girls, put my arms around them, and as they offered a prayer along with mine—Spanish and English, their Catholic prayer to my LDS prayer—as the paramedics rushed in, we watched them put the boy on a stretcher and cover his face with an oxygen mask to help him breathe again.

The girls began shrieking in horror once they heard their brother cry out, thinking he must be slipping away. I hugged them tighter and assured them, "No, that is good. We want him to cry. That means he's breathing. He'll be okay! Your prayers were answered! Thank God Almighty!"

Everyone was crying. The paramedics began rushing the boy away. As the father turned to gather his little ones, he just looked at me as I stood up, and although not a word was spoken, I knew what he was saying through his facial expressions.

"Thank you" sometimes doesn't even need to be said, but it was in the look between fathers.

I'll never know what happened with that little family. We can hope for the best, and I assume all went well upon our parting.

But I'll never forget the feeling of a father telling me "Thank you for helping me and my daughters" without even saying a word.

Sometimes a hug is the only way we can serve. Other times it means getting on a plane and flying to the front lines to give what only we can give. My Signature Moves have taken me across the world and back, delivering smiles and The Promise to those I never imagined would be possible.

## EXERCISE: WHAT IS YOUR PROMISE TO SERVE?

Are your eyes, ears, and heart open to the opportunities all around you to recognize when and where Service is needed?

Take a moment, daily, to recognize who is in need of Service you can render, even if it means picking up garbage while you walk the neighborhood. Keep track of this practice for three days straight and make a game of it with your kids to see who can give the most Service.

When you live this level of Service, there are few ways to feel more peace, joy, and fulfillment.

That is The Promise.

# CHAPTER 8

# MENTORING

*People ask me, "Why is it so hard to trust people?"*
*I ask them, "Why is it so hard to keep a promise?"*

—ANONYMOUS

When I began my career, I reached out to every performer, entertainer, speaker, and hopeful mentor I could imagine, be it someone world-famous or just with niche fame. I was interested in at least one person telling me how they did it and perhaps creating a relationship that could foster Mentoring.

Back then, as us old fellas say, e-mail was quite new, and so I wrote full-page letters and mailed them, along with my VHS tapes, to see who would respond to the budding star I hoped I might be.

During that first round of attempts, not a single, solitary person responded.

So I tried again. Nothing once more.

I then lessened the importance of the fame aspect and went for pretty much anyone in Las Vegas who might respond.

Nada. Zilch.

I was quite surprised and disappointed, as nearly every story I read of the legends from whom I sought to learn had fantastic stories of reaching out to their heroes and being so thrilled to be mentored by them in one way or another.

What I found is that every single one of these stars had received but weren't giving back to the likes of nobodies such as me.

Eventually, I settled on anyone who would be willing to talk to me, from lounge singers I hunted down in person to any act outside of Vegas that I heard about through the rumor mill.

Finally, a few reached out, more from the Q-list of celebrities, and I was fast friends with a few of them as we had much more in common than I would have had with A-listers.

But at the same time, they could tell me only how to get to their level, which, to be frank, I was already knocking at that door to begin my career!

In leadership, and in our Promise to Self, there is the desire to learn, improve, succeed, and hopefully receive help. And equally, we have the responsibility to return the favor when we are the blessed recipient of such.

Mentoring is one of the greatest gifts we can give someone, even if it means a simple phone call just to see if we can help and are the right fit to fill the mentor role.

Having experienced what I did to begin my career, and still to this day finding it challenging to receive mentoring from those I truly wish to learn from, I have made it a personal mantra and active Promise to Self to always mentor in some way with anyone who reaches out.

## THINK FOR A MOMENT OF THE MANY MENTORS IN YOUR LIFE.

Not just those from business and money, but in life! Childhood to college. Mentors abound in my life. While you're thinking of yours, here's a collection of stories to consider some of your earliest mentors and how easy it is for us to make a difference.

"Your son has some, well...challenges," the teacher began.

"Such as?" asked the mother.

"Well, reading is an issue in multiple areas, especially out loud and comprehension. Same with math. The concepts just aren't working in his mind. His writing is compromised and his handwriting is illegible. He seems fine with social skills and making friends, but we are a bit concerned he is doing odd things with his face and mouth, which are distracting to others," she continued.

"What can we do to help him?" the mother inquired.

"We recommend first that you stay after class and assist him in extra reading, or we will need to hold him back. First grade is an excellent time to hold a child back who is struggling or behind. We also recommend a speech therapist, who would double as a psychologist due to some of the issues we are noticing," the teacher concluded.

This may sound like the beginning of the movie *Forrest Gump*, but it was actually my first grade teacher, Ms. Davis, attempting to break it to my Mother that I had a few issues, genetic and learned.

Dang.

So my Mom did what any mother would do: She packed me a sack, put it on the end of a stick, handed me a harmonica, and bid me farewell.

Actually, that's probably what she wanted to do, but instead, since she's an amazing Mom, she came to school every day, became the Homeroom Mom for my entire youth, and sat after class reading with me, making sure I got rid of the challenges of reading, writing, and well, math never panned out, but you can always guess the answers!

Mom taught me by example that this was going to take hard work and her mentoring, her much-needed help. So we tackled it together.

On my Dad's side, he saw there was a problem by about fifth grade when all I was decent at was practicing handwriting and cursive (a much-needed skill today) and drawing. One day he came into my bedroom with a stack of books. He sat next to me on the bed and began his normal sermon-epistle-pep-talk:

"Son, school was very easy for me. I got all good grades, aced every paper, won the spelling bee, all while holding down a few afterschool jobs; practiced basketball, had seven or eight girlfriends, and am a self-taught guitarist. This was before I turned ten. Now that you're that age, I would like to give you the secret to what you really need to know to succeed in life. If you'll read these books, internalize them, and really ponder their meaning, you will succeed beyond that of anyone you know. I know you can. You have it in you, because I'm your father."

He laid out each book before me—

- *As a Man Thinketh* by James Allen

- *How to Win Friends & Influence People* by Dale Carnegie

- *The Greatest Salesman in the World* by Og Mandino

- *The Power of Positive Thinking* by Norman Vincent Peale

- *Think & Grow Rich* by Napoleon Hill

- *Spiritual Roots of Human Relations* by Stephen Covey

At this point I was still trying to get through the *Spot the Dog* series, so this was quite a stretch. But he challenged me anyway and expected an oral report on each book.

I remember that night lying in bed and picking up *The Greatest Salesman in the World*, since I figured my Dad wrote it, but it was by some guy with this cool name—Og Mandino. And I attempted to make it through the first page...something about this salesperson named Hafid and these scrolls I had to read daily before I could even move on to the next page! So I spent the next 30 days reading the First Scroll. Multiple times per day, as prescribed. Reporting to my Dad, who expected me to have it memorized, but little did he realize I could barely remember to turn off the sink when I brushed, so he had to settle for my word that I was really reading it over and over again.

Eventually, I made it through every book—at least, I flipped through the pages looking for pictures—but then something snapped inside of me when I realized my Dad was giving me permission to comprehend these principles and not worry as much about school at this age, and that gave my mind free space to accept these writings.

My Dad taught me, through the example of his self-made career and success, that it just really took hard, smart work. Yes, you'll need a few things to go your way, but be aggressive at times and take risks here and there; just always commit to the work.

Truth is: I was born of goodly parents.

As you read those words, were you thinking of those who have mentored you since the beginning? We all have stories like this of someone who took us under their wing to show us the ropes, whether that be family, teachers, coaches, or friends.

## EXERCISE: MENTOR MEMORY MEMORIAL

With your phone, quickly jot down anyone who comes to mind as a mentor. Consider any family members; friends from early days, high school, and college years; teachers, school counselors, and even those you only saw twice a year (such as my dentist, whom I revere as a mentor of mine in every speech!); people like coaches, community leaders, church teachers, and scout leaders. Now, what about a boss, manager, or someone in the cubicle next to you at your first job? Write all of these down. No order—just write.

I did this exercise when I returned home from serving a mission in Brazil for two years immediately after high school. The memories of mentors came flooding back. Gratitude filled my soul as I thought of people who had made a difference, said a kind word, stayed after school to talk; teachers who saw greatness in me when I didn't see it in myself.

As I wrote down their names, I decided to write them a handwritten letter and hunted down their addresses. This project took me a few hours. Eventually, I mailed the letters off, filled with praise and thanks for those who had helped me.

Months and even years later, I would occasionally run into one of those people who had mentored me, either in small or profound ways, short stints or long periods of time. Each person threw their arms around me as if to greet a long lost friend. Each said it was a life-defining moment for them to realize their mentoring had made a difference through my letter they had received. I remember being quite stunned, as I thought I was just being kind by letting them know what they had done for me.

In reality, a majority of those to whom I had written letters had never in their lives received a letter of thanks like that, be it from a student, a friend, or a work colleague.

I encourage you to do something similar. Get out some stationary, go buy a few blank cards, and sit and write Mentor Memory Memorials. Send them. It very well may change the life of the person receiving it. Promise me you will do this.

Now you have reached out to those who influenced you. I hope it feels wonderful to share the gift of Gratitude with those who gave to you when you were just figuring life out.

At this point, you may be thinking of those in your work, in your home, and in the community who may need mentoring or perhaps have reached out to you asking for advice.

If you know the story of Leonardo da Vinci, you know that he was an illegitimate son, born in the town of Vinci, Italy, to a family of notaries. His mind never would have worked well in that profession, and he was dropped off at the workshop of a famous sculptor, and sometimes painter, Verrocchio in Florence, Italy, to live and apprentice for his schooling.

Legend has it that one day, as was common for a busy workshop, a painting needed to be finished quickly and Leonardo was told to paint an angel in the corner. Upon seeing Leonardo's angel on the painting, originally nearly completed by Verrocchio, the expert artist stood in shock and said, "I will never paint again having seen Leonardo's ability next to mine."

This teacher should be praised, for he then went from teacher to mentor to Leonardo, who eventually became considered the most gifted painter of all time, giving him every opportunity and chance to become what the teacher recognized was greatness beyond his own.

## WHO ARE YOU MENTORING? WHERE ARE THE OPPORTUNITIES TO DO SO?

This is The Promise of helping others to CLARIFY and MAGNIFY their gifts, even when it may mean they could be greater than yours. It seems to be a natural tendency for parents to want to mentor their children; however, in some instances, it is either neglected due to a busy life or can even fall into an odd jealousy that forever divides the family when a child outshines the parent. It is rare for a mentor to be so invested in the success of the mentee that they do anything they can to help them succeed, even if they become greater than their mentor. But that is what true Mentoring is, and that is where the story of Verrocchio is impressive in regard to Leonardo.

Are you the type of mentor who creates opportunities for your mentee to soar higher than you did?

*A true mentor develops their mentee's gifts, even if it means the mentee surpasses the mentor.*

My father's profession was life insurance and financial planning. He and I assumed I would join the family business upon becoming an adult. However, I quickly realized that it wasn't for me, I had no gift in the field, and I had a passion for being an artist, singer, performer, entertainer, and speaker.

My Mom would cover for me as I stayed up all night working on my act, for fear that approaching my Dad with this idea of my becoming a performer would be a waste of the $50,000 high school education granted me.

I'll never forget handing him a demo CD I had cut singing in my own voice some of his favorite songs while I played the piano and even added in a few funny voices. He went into his office—this man who had sold over a billion dollars in life insurance and built an empire of success. His shadow loomed large over my life, and I paced nervously in the front entryway of our 12,000-square foot mansion as I heard my Dad play my CD not just once, but again and again and again.

Terrified as he opened the door, I saw him walk toward me...with tears in his eyes.

"This is you? Your voice is so wonderful, your performance astounding. You really want to do this instead of work with me?" he asked.

"Yes, Dad, I really think I have what it takes to make a living from the stage," I proclaimed.

He said, "Well then, what do you need? I will do anything I can, open any door, to help. Just be the best in the world."

Woah.

My fear of his acceptance of me wanting to follow my dream was all unfounded. He just needed to know what I wanted and that I was serious, and he could hear on the CD that I probably could make a go at it.

He then joined forces with the mentors who had helped me cut the demo in studio, had led me to a point where I could approach my father, and had gotten me gigs without him knowing. It was a covert operation of mentors helping me get the blessing of the person I needed it from the most.

My Dad opened his book of contacts, which included the Who's Who of business in America. If I were to say I just happened to create all of my business and life, the financial success achieved on my own, that would be an outright lie. My Dad opened the door, and I ran through it with all the might of a man starving for success, to prove not only to myself, but to his clients, that he was right.

Before I knew it, I was flying to Las Vegas to audition for the biggest opportunity of my life, with the Las Vegas *Legends in Concert* show, where more mentors became a part of the story of my success and life—people like Cully Davis, Johnny Stewart, Steve McCoy, Kenny Barrett, all leading me to the first of many levels of progression.

Suddenly, I found myself standing onstage between the 7:00 P.M. and 9:30 P.M. shows, having just watched the greatest impersonators in the world, and I got 15 minutes while the room was turned over for the next crowd at the Imperial Palace on the Strip, as I performed my routines of Jim Carrey as a Subway sandwich artist, Billy Joel as Piano Man, Alvin & The Chipmunks, and dancing like Michael Jackson for the less than ten people looking on. A few funny faces here, a dentist's office sound effects routine there, and by the end of my quick act the owner of the show, the famous legend of showbiz Johnny Stewart, yelled up to me, "Can you do a Ricky Martin impression?" I shook my hips and smiled as I chopped through an impromptu "Livin' La Vida Loca."

"I need you by June to be our Ricky Martin for the show in Myrtle Beach!" he announced. Problem was, I was getting married in June and would not be home from my honeymoon until July 1.

"July 1 then," he said. "This is your big break, kid. Don't let us down."

I was 22 years old, a month away from getting married. I'd just landed the opportunity of a lifetime going from making $100 per one-off gig, if I was lucky to land any, to now a steady paycheck at

$1,200 per week as a newlywed performing daily in a Las Vegas production. I couldn't wait to tell my soon-to-be bride that our dreams were coming true.

Question once again: Who are your mentors? Who are you mentoring?

My Dad took a chance in opening his contacts list. His contacts took a chance flying me to Vegas in their private jet. The show owner gave me a chance to perform and see what I could do.

All mentors. Anyone can be a mentor if they think like one. Or we can just let every opportunity to help, coach, train, and give back just pass on by.

## EXERCISE: BECOMING THE MENTOR: THE CHRIS POULOS EFFECT

Who can you mentor?

Make your list.

Perhaps it's just one person. Maybe they even live with you and they're your child...whoever you decide it is, who will you mentor? Someone you work with, manage? Perhaps a neighbor or your best friend's kid who wants to be like you? You decide.

Those who mentor naturally made a subconscious Promise to be a mentor many moons ago. They appreciated the influence someone else had on them, and when they see potential, or a desire from someone they can teach, they jump at the chance to mentor.

Write down the name, or names, of someone you will mentor.

One more story and we will close—

How did I get that demo CD made that helped convince my father I was a singer? This is my most important mentor story of them all.

The greatest mentor of my adult life had been introduced to me by my former basketball coach turned life mentor, Coach Tony Ingle. Coach Ingle had seen me at the BYU basketball summer camps during my high school years. He saw my determination to make it to the NBA. He sat me down between my junior and senior year of high school and said,

"Son, I'd like to offer you a full-ride scholarship to BYU."

I was stunned. "Me? I'm not even that great at basketball."

He smiled. "Jason," he said in his southern drawl, "You are the funniest person I've ever seen. The things you can do with your face, voice, as a singer—I've never seen anyone like you. You are the kind of person we want on the team, on the bus, at the practice, pushing the players to get better and making us laugh. We aren't giving you a scholarship to play, although you'll play with the team in practice; we're giving you a full ride to be funny and be here with us!"

Now I was offended. My dream was to play in the NBA, but Coach Ingle was telling me I was funny and that's what he saw in me. He could tell I was confused.

"Young man," he continued, "you've become a very good basketball player by sheer grit and determination. If you apply yourself to entertaining others like you have to being an athlete, you will be famous and on stages worldwide for the rest of your life. I can see it! Do you believe that?"

I wasn't so sure. I went away from that camp confused and even hurt. I didn't follow up on the offer. I didn't stay in touch with the coach.

A few years later, as an adult, I ran into Coach Ingle again. His life had taken its turns, as had mine, and he asked me if I was pursuing my performing career. I told him I was going to work for my Dad. Coach Ingle looked at me and said, "You should be onstage young man. Let me introduce you to the guy who will make it happen..."

Enter Chris Poulos.

He was 75; I was 21. Luke Skywalker meets Yoda. Chris had managed nationally touring artists and produced shows for 35 years, as well as programmed speaking events for nearly 50, with the likes of Stephen Covey and others. Chris was a legend in the business, and upon being introduced to me by Coach Ingle, I showed him some of my funny routines, voices, and songs.

Chris and I immediately connected. I spent hours in his living room as he mentored me to the point of landing my first events, my first paid gigs, putting together my promotional materials, all while keeping me working, creating, and being my first manager.

He never took a penny. Still hasn't to this day. I would spend between four to eight hours with him every other day for my first year with him, as he taught me everything from negotiations in showbiz, to how to promote, connect, network, spin opportunities, showcase, create my act, discover my philosophy, confirm my intention, and infused me with confidence.

He opened his contact book and gave me every opportunity that led to everything good that would create my career.

And then he brought me to the studio, where we recorded the demo, which I handed to my Dad, and which eventually led to the next level of doors being opened.

## A MENTOR'S INFLUENCE IS EXPONENTIAL.

Chris has stood on only a few stages, and he's quite funny and an incredible teacher and speaker, but he hasn't performed for millions of people.

But actually, yes, yes he has. Through his mentoring of me he has. And now, 20 years later, in his 90s, we still talk philosophy and spiritual guidance and mentoring on a weekly basis.

Without Chris Poulos, you would never have heard of me, unless I was trying to sell you insurance in a job I would be very bummed having settled on as my life's path.

Without Chris Poulos, I would not be standing on stages for money because I wouldn't know how.

Without Chris Poulos, I would never have gotten my foot in any door, off any ground.

Chris made a Promise as a young 20-something-year-old that if someone had talent and wanted to make a go of it in showbiz, he would help get them in front of an audience.

Who will you mentor?

I call this The Chris Poulos Effect.

Don't mentor for money. Don't do it for fame, acknowledgment, or recognition.

Mentor because it's part of who you are. It's your Legacy to the world.

Mentor because it's Your Promise.

# CHAPTER 9

# HEALTH

*Keep every promise you make
and only make promises you can keep.*

—ANTHONY HITT

Every morning, without fail, the lights go on in our living room before 7:00 A.M. No, it's not an automatic timer, and no, it's not me up that early most days. It's our 11-year-old boy doing 1,000 sit-ups. Once again, he's 11.

This didn't begin as a dare, and I don't pay him to do this. He just wakes up every morning and goes to work forming his perfect preteen washboard abs. He has done this now for over two years. We have no idea where this child came from, although we are very proud.

When you're a kid, you begin molding the shape of your life directly through your Habits, Patterns, and Promises. Yes, you will change some, but in reality, most often what you create by the time you're outside of that first decade will stick with you for life, to some degree. Just look at your Habits and try to pinpoint when they began.

Healthy living is a Promise to Self. Yes, you must be selfish enough to take care of your Health in order to be there for everyone else.

I have spoken with men on their deathbeds who have proclaimed, "I spent my entire youth sacrificing my Health in order to build my wealth. Now in my aging years, I would spend all of my wealth to reclaim my Health!"

Of all the chapters written in this book, this is the one on which I feel most unqualified to be an authority and speak about. Perhaps this entire chapter is simply about my broken Promises of Health to myself.

I know very few people who have experienced the swings in weight, body fat, and dieting like I have. If you've tried everything, I could probably one-up you, but what is the point in that? Needless to say, if you've been there, then we understand one another's pain.

The Promise pertaining to Health is the one that literally shows on your body and manifests your true Promise to it. Think of it: Integrity can be feigned until found out, Habits hidden, Service rendered without joy but still accomplished...on and on. Yet Health physically shows.

I have found myself in the midst of a 30–60 cycle of perfect eating, weighing my food, killing it at the gym, sweating a new level of crazy while my trainer screams at me, depriving my body of all that it desires and wants while going to bed completely depressed having just downed a broccoli shake in my effort to stay afloat.

Within days of my attempt at perfection, I will find myself waking up from a sleepwalking, binge-movie-watching zombie state, having eaten 2.5 bags of chips and every top off the muffins in the pantry. The crash is brutal, the extreme dieting having never become my new "lifestyle"—an unattainable mess.

If you're judging me while reading this and yelling at the page, "Stop crash dieting! Do something that works!" the truth is, with my genetic makeup and travel schedule, only drastic measures can move the needle of my natural disposition. We all have our cross to bear. This is mine. What's yours?

## Why set a Goal when we can make a Promise?

I religiously would go to the gym, consult trainers and programs, spend tens of thousands of dollars in gimmicks, tests, shakes, gym memberships, and the like. I lose 10 pounds here, 20 pounds there, swing back up to 25 pounds over, and then go back on down—over and over for 20 years now. Crazy to think this has been the bane of my existence and greatest destroyer of my confidence.

When I force myself to do something, to eat a certain way only, to go to the gym and squeeze a workout in, I can only sustain this effort so long. Even as I make the Promises I've made in the past—that once I hit that ideal weight I am never going back, never eating that old way again—like clockwork I find myself where I began just weeks or months before.

This is the new normal for most people in America. We all try so hard. New Year's resolutions and gym memberships are like a running joke to most of our society regarding the weight we're going to take off this time!

This is where Goals and Promises come into play in the most meaningful way you may ever realize.

I like to say, "Why set a Goal when we can make a Promise?"

You may have also remembered I say, "Goals are Particulars where Promises are Proclamations."

> *Goals are Particulars*
> *where Promises are Proclamations.*

Here's the difference.

You set a Goal to lose weight, you make small Goals to eat a certain way, and you reach (or almost do) that Goal.

You hit the mark, you did it! Goal accomplished!

However, a Goal seems to have a deadline, an end zone, a "we got here, now let's rest" idea to it.

And then there's a Promise.

IF I make a Promise, it is that commitment, plain and simple.

Instead of just setting the Goal to lose weight, imagine it's a Promise to do whatever it takes to get there.

Instead of just setting the Goal to get to the gym every day, imagine it's a Promise to get there every day as part of your lifestyle.

Once your thinking shifts from having Goals that need to be accomplished, with a timeline and deadline, to Promises that are just what they are, that's when the whole game is altered.

As I write this, I have just made another huge swing in my weight, fat percentage, and lifestyle. Over the past six months, I have lost (and kept off) 10 to 12 pounds, with my body fat down 2 to 3 percent. That is doable to maintain because of my Promise.

What is my Promise and secret?

I bought a new wardrobe.

Kidding! Well, sort of.

My Promise is quite simple and very practicable, compared to the Goals and restrictions I imposed upon myself for the past two decades.

## MY HEALTH PROMISE IS A PROCLAMATION TO SELF.

I sweat every single day, be it in a walk, run, hike, or rigorous workout that makes me happy.

Not only is this for my own enjoyment, but it releases the endorphins I need to create, write, and become better in my profession.

I only eat that which makes me feel wonderful, with no repercussions.

I'm welcome to enjoy a treat of sugar or white carbs, but I will pay a price called misery, since I am allergic to those foods.

My Health Promise is my example to my family that what I do is more important than what I say, that my body is my Temple and speaks for itself, and that I can do any physical activity anyone else can do, no matter my age.

Added bonus: I LOVE the way I look and feel, especially watching videos of myself on the stage and not hiding behind my clothing.

So, here is your Health Promise Exercise for this chapter:

## EXERCISE: CREATE YOUR HEALTH PROMISE PROCLAMATION

If that means you set little goals, the particulars, that get you to that point, then go for it. And as you plan those out, come up with your own Health Promise.

My boy, Romney, the 11-year-old workout machine I described at the beginning of the chapter, made a Promise to himself a few years ago regarding his own Health Proclamation, and he came to it naturally.

His intention is to become a professional basketball player. So he's starting now. He doesn't eat sugar, refuses anything bad for his body, does his full workouts morning and night, and will not go to sleep without cranking it out, no matter how tired or late it is. We have eaten the world's greatest frozen custard, had Disneyland desserts, and enjoyed movie snacks with him seated next to us, refusing to indulge in any of the treats.

He's incredible. I've never seen a kid with this sort of willpower. But it's part of his Life Promise, and he's sticking to it. I only wish I were so determined.

What is your level of commitment to your Health Promise Proclamation?

Now, if you're comfortable wandering down the rabbit hole with me, let's go deeper.

The Health Promise Proclamation is only Round 1. Speaking these words, proclaiming and ingraining these words and Promises, can only get us so far.

Even if the doctor tells you that your eating and Health habits are going to kill you—that even one pizza might do you in—for a majority of us this isn't enough. I have even known people with diabetes who are told they are going to die if they don't stop eating sugar, and they've told me this story over ice cream.

Don't get me wrong, this is human nature and the physical man versus the spiritual. It is our test in this life, our agency, our willpower, our capacity to give our bodies the best we can—even when we don't want or care to.

# MY BROKEN PROMISE

My entire life I didn't drink caffeine until I discovered energy drinks about five years ago. If you've seen the science and research on this stuff, it's about as damning a product as someone can subject themselves to that is currently considered allowable to consume, even though it may be as dangerous as drugs.

I have known that I should wean myself of this habit of energy drinks, and I can do so for a month at a time, and then I go right back to it.

Even when I make Promises to myself to stop, I can stick with it only for about three to four weeks max, which is historically, according to the experts, the amount of time needed to create a new Habit. Not so with a real addiction.

And then I flew to Malaysia for an event.

In my effort to fight jetlag, after flying for 26 hours to get there, I needed to remain awake for my speech to 5,000 financial planners. So I drank my sugarless energy drink mix I brought along with me. A few hours later, I downed another one. A few hours later, I found an energy drink in the mini fridge in my room. Guzzled it. I know I'm not supposed to drink too many of these because it can cause you harm. Even at this point a Promise wasn't enough.

I did my sound check for the event the next day; walked around the city in its heat and humidity; enjoyed some of the spicy foods; ate durian, the king of fruits that smells like a sewer but tastes like heaven; and then I went back to my hotel room at 4:00

P.M., needing to remain awake until 8:00 P.M. to go to sleep and get my body on time for the next day's speech.

I drew a bath, hoping to ease my sore body, poured myself a Diet Pepsi, and slithered into the tub. I never take baths. I never just sit and drink soda. But about 15 minutes into my soak, I felt the need to get out of the tub and into my robe. Then I got in bed and began watching a movie, with three hours left to stay awake.

That's when my heart did this thing.

I'd never felt anything like it before.

It didn't hurt, but it felt unnatural, like it was skipping a beat or fluttering.

I looked around. I paused the movie. I heard the construction from outside my Ritz Carlton room on the 17th floor of the high-rise.

Flutter. Flutter. Pounce. Beat, stop, beat, flutter, bump, bump.

My heart has never done anything close to this.

Back home it was the middle of the night. No way was I calling my wife to tell her I think I'm having a heart attack...in Malaysia.

Fearful to alarm anyone about my situation, as I still had to speak the next morning, I did what anyone would do who isn't sure of the best thing to do.

I stood up slowly, unlocked my hotel room door, took the "Do Not Disturb" sign off the handle, and left the main locks off.

Do you know what I was doing?

I was allowing easy entry for whoever might find me to enter and take my body away.

I wrote a note and set it on the side of my bed with the explanation:

"I think I drank too much caffeine after all of my flights. I took a warm bath, and that didn't help. My wife's name is Tami. This is her number. We live in Utah. Please give this note to my family.

"My Family, I'm sorry. I love you and will miss you. Daddy."

And I closed my eyes as my heart danced to a rhythm it had never matched.

I figured I was going to die.

Why didn't I call for emergency assistance? I figured it would be better for my client to find me passed away than miss the gig due to being in the hospital.

I guess when you're in another country, hyped on caffeine, and sleep deprived, you think weird thoughts. Writing it now it sounds completely insane and absurd. But that's what I did.

Where do you come into this story?

Have you ever done or thought something like this?

Whether yes or no, imagine it for a moment.

What Promises do you believe I made while lying in a hotel room in Malaysia thinking I'm going to die? I made some Promises to myself, to God.

# "LET ME LIVE AND I'LL..."

I'll what?

We do this all the time.

"Spare me this moment, this pain, this horrible thing I'm going through, and I promise you, God, I will be a changed person."

How often do you keep that Promise?

My point exactly.

We are all Promise Makers and Breakers.

Do you think I drank an energy drink the next day when I really, really needed one?

No, the fear of what had happened 18 hours earlier was too much for me.

And no, I didn't drink another energy drink or any caffeine all the way home either, which was actually really difficult to do.

I landed and was so thankful to be home. As I raced to my house, I was so tired I couldn't believe it.

And I remembered my Promise. "I will not drink those drinks, or any caffeine, anymore." I said it to myself out loud...

As I pulled into the gas station.

As I walked into the building.

As I picked my poison from the assortment of options.

As I paid for it.

I kept repeating over and over in my mind that I wouldn't do it, that I had made a Promise to myself.

As I cracked the energy drink can open in my car and began to drink.

I felt refreshed and happy to have my drink again and felt equally like I was the greatest hypocrite on planet Earth, a planet I thought I'd be leaving a few days earlier due to my Habit of drinking excessive energy drinks. I'd sworn off this Habit, and here I was drinking one again.

When The Promise isn't enough, even after thinking you're going to die, even when the doctor tells you that you must stop a behavior, even when your family is suffering, or as you're suffering what you think is a heart attack in Malaysia, then what is the real answer?

This is Level 2, or Round 2, of The Promise.

This is you pulling the paddles off the wall and shocking your heart to start it up again after you've fallen to the ground in foolishness, in addiction, in succumbing to the lures of body over spirit.

That Promise is passionate engagement in a purpose, mission, or project so powerful that not even your greatest vices have power over it.

That Promise is called The Promise Legacy Project.

Imagine for a moment that you know you have one week left on earth. That's it. Time's up at that point. What do you leave as your Legacy? You have one week to figure it out!

The Promise Legacy Project overpowers addiction, overcomes obsession and ignorance, and instead replaces that which has ruled your existence with something more powerful than all powers controlling you.

You have one shot. One life. One moment. You are falling from the sky, you are pulling the cord on the parachute, but you know it's lights out as soon as that chute doesn't open.

What is your Promise Legacy Project? That which you leave to this world?

This, for me, is the only strategy strong enough to will me to live at my highest level of engagement with the present, plan for my best future, and do what's best for me and my Health now.

For some people it may just be the thought of your children needing you, your words being left behind, your photos and videos in order, or work being accomplished.

But this Promise Legacy Project is my answer to healthy living, when the Health Promise Proclamation isn't strong enough.

I can say it all day long, but I need a higher purpose, a greater reason, and that's The Promise Legacy Project.

Want to know what mine is?

To be a father, able-bodied, fully aware, for my little ones.

To write this book, and the many more I have in me.

To live my Legacy and not just leave a Legacy.

What are yours? What would drive you to actually living a healthy life?

There are unicorns among us who never need to go this deep— they just eat healthy, they work out daily, they only drink

Kombucha and sing "Kumbaya" around campfires and post about their trips to Costa Rica with their families.

Those are real people, and good for them—they've conquered this aspect already and have won at life.

But the fact is, a majority of every person on earth is struggling with something along the lines of that which I have just disclosed to you is my struggle.

Read mine, acknowledge and state yours, take courage that we all face it, and now create your life.

Manifest what it looks like. Staring death in the face is one way, but for some it's not enough. So instead, consider that which you are meant for, the unfinished business you have left to give this world—the music unrecorded, the memories yet to be made— and become obsessed about making it happen.

That is your Promise Legacy Project. There is nothing in life like this level of commitment. And you will overcome your greatest trials and challenges once you make this Promise.

What's yours?

# CHAPTER 10

# GOD

---

*I've learned that when God promises
beauty through the ashes, He means it.*

—TAYA KYLE

In my world, God is very real. If you don't have the same belief, I still encourage you to read this chapter, as you can liken this to a higher power, nature, humanity, and in general something bigger and greater than you. I will utilize the language of "God," though, for this chapter.

The first time I stood on a stage and presented "The Promise," I had divided the speech into three sections:

- The Promise to The Audience (your customers)

- The Promise to The Family (at work and at home), and

- The Promise to The One.

Everyone in the audience later told me they assumed I was going to talk about God as The One. I found that fascinating since this was a corporate event where God is not mentioned a majority of the time due to the fear of bringing "religion" into the conversation.

The sense in which I speak here, please know that religion has nothing to do with God. Religion is simply a way to discover and remain close to eternity, but it is only the tip of the iceberg.

I espouse the thought of something much greater and grander than me, not just to believe in, but to put my cards and whole hand on the table to be all in.

My Promise to God is the single most important aspect of my life. How do we identify what that Promise really is? We simply have to take a real, true, frank assessment of our view of life and our place in it.

*We have to take a frank assessment of our view of life and our place in it.*

Imagine yourself sitting on a porch, with the perfect amount of sunshine, a soft cool breeze, the sound of tree leaves clapping together, a bird chirping, the sweet scent of a flower in full bloom or a neighbor grilling some delicious ribs, and the taste of your favorite drink.

Peace washes over you.

It is the kind of feeling where breathing in deeply reminds you of your full Gratitude for life.

You are calm, yet self-assured. You may be reading, writing, or just looking into the distance at the ocean, or mountains, or the grassy baseball field where a Dad and his son play catch.

It's in these moments that you find a deep connection with God, in your silent prayer of Gratitude for the life which has been given to you. These are moments of reflection and introspection that confirm your resolve to live the life you promised yourself you would.

What are your Promises to God?

Think of His Promises to you!

He promises His spirit, comfort, and joy will wash over you as you keep your Promises.

So, what are your Promises to God?

One of the ways I remember my Promise to God is the acronym G.O.D.

- G = Gifts
- O = Obedience
- D = Discipleship

The following are examples of living and committing to each.

## GIFTS

You have gifts that must be discovered, cultivated, and shared. Are you sharing your gifts?

You have been given opportunities to do amazing things, to serve others, and to be a person of influence as only you can.

## The Promise to God
## is never to waste the gift.

The gift of time, the gift of serving, the gift of making a difference.

My Promise is broken to God when I blatantly miss the mark and hold back my gifts, which happens the most when I deny those who ask for my help or for Service. This sense of purpose to give back has driven my entire life's work.

The next level of a broken Promise to God for me is when I do Service but with a feeling of anger or guilt associated with it.

For example: Many years ago, I was asked to perform my very physically demanding, time-consuming, and challenging show for a group that had claimed it would put me in front of all the right people to further my career. The only catch was they had no money to pay me.

If you've been in showbiz, you know the claim that it's for "exposure" is perhaps the most commonly used excuse from someone needing a favor or just too cheap to pay you.

What those people don't realize is that people in the wild die of "exposure," which is the most repulsive word to the entrepreneur and usually doesn't work.

However, this was a friend, and they needed my help. Service to God, that was my Promise, so I went and put on a huge show.

As the evening proceeded, I realized that I had been "had." The setting was a country club for wealthy golfers; the meal was a six-course lobster and steak extravaganza; they gave away overnight stays at the best hotels, ski trips to Aspen and Park City; and then it was my turn to perform my show after not even being offered a chance to eat, after my crew and I had also rented a sound system and lights to provide for them in their "desperate need."

Feeling completely taken advantage of, in my Service to God and in turn to Self, I still gave an outstanding performance, delivered my all, and shared my gift with the audience of mostly unappreciative, unresponsive, disinterested onlookers.

And then I broke my Promise to God. After my show was over and as the crowd began clearing out, I became angry at the client, the crowd, and myself for accepting this farce of an event. I gathered my costumes, lifted heavy speakers and lights to put them in cases, and bent down to begin wrapping cords.

My sullen and negative attitude began infiltrating the entire room and experience, and soon my crew and the guys I'd hired out of my own money to help me began to put on the same vibe I had.

All of us simmered in disappointment that this evening hadn't panned out as we had hoped. We knew exposure simply meant dying in front of a bad audience, and this was our own "Truman Show" experience, as we perished in the desert of sand and sadness.

A lady came over to me and tried to talk with me. I gave her no time. I didn't even look at her; I just kept wrapping my cords with the intention of getting out of there to go grab a cheap meal at Wendy's.

She said, "Excuse me, young man."

I ignored her.

She tried again, "Hello there...can I have a minute to tell you something?"

I looked up from my bent knee, annoyed out of my mind that now I have to talk to the people who don't care about me and have just taken advantage of me. *Just let me leave!* I screamed inside.

She could tell I was not interested in chatting, so she put her arm on my shoulder and said, "May I tell you something?"

I was now in full get-out-of-my-face, feeling-sorry-for-myself, angry-and-becoming-depressed mode as I looked up at her, eyes nearly rolling to the back of my head with full physical disinterest painted all over.

"Yes?" I exhaled.

"I just wanted to tell you thank you for the laughs tonight," she said, so proud of her kind compliment.

*Of course she laughed,* I thought, *everyone laughed, and I am the butt of this evening.*

I forced a smile and said, "That's wonderful," and went back to wrapping my cords.

Now she had had it. She wasn't going to let me get away with not taking her compliment, and of course I knew better than to treat another person this way, but I was so ticked off, so upset about the evening, I just couldn't fake it anymore. Yet she still came at me.

Now she grabbed me by my shoulders with both hands and squared me up while looking me in the eyes, as she determinedly stated, "I want to thank you for making me laugh today, young man!" She was adamant that this was high praise, although I heard it every day, so I forced a bigger smile and said, "That's very great."

She then said something that forever changed my life. Looking deep into my soul, she proclaimed, "You making me laugh is a miracle, and the miracle I needed this very day. You see, I have been crying my eyes out all day at home, and I dragged myself to attend this event tonight, in pain, in sorrow, in agony. My doctor told me today that I am diagnosed with M.S. and will not live much longer. You are my angel this day. Thank you for healing my soul by making me laugh."

And she fell into my arms sobbing.

I had broken a Promise to God, and in turn, humanity, by not pushing past my ego of feeling disappointed by this evening and the Promises made to me that were broken. And even as I still delivered the show, I had forgotten my Promise always to love all people no matter how horrible I felt in the moment about my current state of being disrespected and disappointed.

And here was a woman trying to thank me for the gift I had delivered to her, as an angel in her time of need for healing, and I had made it very hard for her to share her sacred expression of thanks.

That was a broken Promise by me to God.

What is the first and greatest commandment?

Love God.

And the next?

Love thy neighbor as thyself.

I had broken The Promise, even after keeping The Promise by showing up and doing my service, my charity...and then ego got the best of me.

> ## My Promise to God is to be love to all, to spread joy to all, to be accepting to all.

This is not a choice dependent upon whether people can further my career, or if they lie to me, disappoint me, and make me feel worthless, which I felt at this event and have at so many before, after, and since.

Yet in this moment, this woman having just been diagnosed with a death sentence helped me put it all back into perspective.

It doesn't matter if we show up and do the service—if our pride gets in the way, if we are worried about what we'll get out of it, if we're put out for not getting the credit we deserve, that is The Promise broken to God.

What is your Promise to God in sharing your gifts? Because they're not yours; they're His.

## OBEDIENCE

At 19 years of age, most men are headed to college, the military, working part-time, and/or chasing every girl in town.

When I turned 19, I was packing to move to Brazil to be a missionary for two years. Allowed two phone calls home per year on Mother's Day and Christmas, armed with teachings I believed could help others and intentions to learn a language completely foreign to me, I would serve the people and have no admittance to date, touch, or even hug the opposite sex.

Having saved money my entire life for this experience and been taught the lessons I would teach, I was grateful for a family that supported and loved me and was proud of my commitment.

When I was a boy, I made a Promise to become a missionary someday, and every dart from the adversary was thrown to divert this mission; yet here I was, ready to serve.

Obedience is a habit, a choice, a value, and one of God's great tests to see about our fortitude and Promise to Him.

What does Obedience to God look like in your life?

Perhaps it's not as drastic as leaving home to live in a Third World country and knocking on doors all day in the heat and humidity while speaking Portuguese, but maybe it is doing little things consistently, such as waking up grateful, treating your body with respect by what you feed it, and filling your mind with scripture and positive thoughts as opposed to the simpler news of the day and social media feed.

As you consider your Obedience to God in living The Promise, think back on the times you've felt a small voice tell you to do something, to make a phone call to an old friend or parent, and the result as to whether you followed through or not. If you did it, then you know the feeling of comfort and peace in following through on a prompting. If you didn't, you know the sorrow that comes with disconnecting from that small voice upon knowing you should have done what you felt.

Back to Brazil. Paired with another young man who was also learning the language, in our white shirts and ties we wandered the streets in search of anyone who might listen to our message of joy and happiness. Few gave us a chance. To the buses we went... where my life took a significant turn.

Mass transit in small cities in southern Santa Catarina, Brazil, means buses full of tired workers headed long distances back and forth from their rural homes to the city, making for a belabored existence, where the bus is essentially one's only comfort if a seat can be found.

As we entered the bus, my companion and I realized only he could find a seat, so I stood in the back, as person after person, tired and downtrodden, entered the bus to fill the aisle, standing and swaying as the bus hobbled along cobblestones and then dirt roads over hills and through valleys.

Looking at these strangers, I felt compassion beyond any I had experienced in my life to that point. I could see emptiness and sorrow in their faces, coupled with sadness and nearly expiring energy, and I began to ask God if there would be something I could do for any of them, other than our routine of knocking on one door at a time to hopefully share our message.

In deep thought, I heard a voice, felt it deep in my heart, that said,

"Sing."

I looked around to see who was talking to me. No one had. Again it said the same thing:

"Sing."

That is when I realized what this was—it was the voice that the prophets of old and disciples had heard in their hearts for millennia. It was God telling me what needed to be done for His children on that bus.

As sudden as the sound and thought entered my heart, so did the doubt, fear, and absolute ridiculousness in terms of reason that combated the word.

"Why would I sing? On a bus? These people don't want someone singing to them! I don't even speak their language well enough yet—I don't even know a song in Portuguese all the way through!"

When was the last time you had this type of dialogue, when you've felt that voice telling you what to do—whether it was encouraging you to apologize to someone you have done wrong, or to make a left turn instead of a right, even to stop and help a person on the side of the road? This is what God does to test our Promise of Obedience to Him.

As I battled my own thought versus that which was put inside my mind, I realized the language of song needs no translation; I could sing a hymn in English that they would know and it would still be edifying to them.

Courage welled up in me, my eyes darting back and forth, observing the state of every person; my companion seated, reading his scriptures on a bench. As if the gates opened to a den of lions, I released the song in my heart as I raised my voice, along with my eyes and body, to announce to the bus from the back:

"Excuse me! I am a missionary of Jesus Christ and I would like to sing you a song!"

Tired and confused, the passengers turned annoyed eyes to see the crazy American in the back, standing and now preaching on the bus. I broke into song:

"How Great Thou Art!"

"Oh Lord my God, when I in awesome wonder, consider all the worlds thy hands have made..."

Singing and raising my voice, the entire bus fell silent; tears began streaming down the faces of weary travelers, music filling an old rickety bus and entering the hearts of the listeners.

As I finished, "How Great Thou Art! How Great Thou Art!" the entire bus burst into applause. My companion sat, confused and embarrassed, watching this spectacle, but he seemed as pleased as I was that it was received with such enthusiasm.

We then began working the crowd, walking through the bus as people hugged me and shook my hand, telling me it was beautiful and inquiring if I would be singing on the bus again tomorrow. I asked if we could come to their house to teach them of our important message of happiness...

Every person told me the same thing:

"No."

But they said they liked the song.

After talking with and inviting every person on the bus to hear our message, we exited at a rural stop without thinking, as the show was over and a random stop was our backstage to hide from the audience. My companion looked at me and asked,

"Did anyone want us to come to their home to teach them?"

I replied, "No. Every single person said 'no.' I thought God told me to sing, so I did, but I guess it was just my mind telling me and not Him."

As my companion and I began walking the miles home we had left, I felt horrible. Deflated. Defeated. Why had I done such a thing, a spectacle, and it hadn't resulted in anything we anticipated?

It wasn't until that night as I slept that I received the answer.

Obedience to The Voice doesn't have to be rewarded immediately; in fact, it rarely is. It is acting upon the impression felt inside that proves your Obedience, which allows for greater trust and responsibility the next time.

The Promise to God is Obedience, whether it yields results now or later. It is all a test. It is all to further how often He can guide you and see if you'll follow regardless of the reward.

This is proven in scripture from Abraham confusedly holding his only son down to sacrifice to Moses finally convincing Pharaoh to let his people go, only to come up against The Red Sea with nowhere to go with the Egyptian army chasing them down. Obedience is The Promise of the prophets and true followers of God.

I realized that God had tested me, my courage, my faith, my obedience to do something absolutely not on script. He rewarded me later, as He does nearly every time, with opportunities and blessings that few can comprehend, in bringing His message to people who were waiting to listen but needed it told by someone in a way that only I could deliver it.

Had I never lifted my voice on that bus, I would never know what my life would have missed, but I know the richness of His blessings stem from that moment, and His trust to send opportunities and moments my way came from that pivotal, life-changing event.

As you reflect on your life, the times you have felt The Voice in your mind and heart telling you what to do, to act, to create, to not have fear but to trust in something greater than you, even God, how have you been obedient to your Promise?

If you are regretting it now, have no sadness; just make a resolution that you will act upon it the next time, and then pray mightily for the opportunity to prove yourself.

God rewards your Obedience, tests your Promise, and will challenge your fortitude. Want proof? Read the Book of Job. Then jump to The Acts.

If you are living a life of mediocrity and are lacking direction, understand the will of God and commit to Obedience. Listen to The Voice that will say what to do—a Voice that is quiet, still, small, and yet you know is right, in giving you chances to serve, to risk, to lift, to live The Promise!

## DISCIPLESHIP

The word derives from *discipline*.

The Disciples were followers and teachers of the word of God.

Discipline, however, has become fully misconstrued in becoming a negative, in the sense of:

"I disciplined my child for doing what was not right." Or, "We must take disciplinary action for your behavior."

What is forgotten is that discipline also carries the great definition on the highest end of positivity of one working toward perfecting a craft, such as the discipline of learning a musical instrument, an artist laboring over her masterpiece, or a hard worker putting in overtime to advance his career.

In my life, I have comically messed up my perspective on Discipleship in favor of the negative.

Learning early on that blessings are predicated upon our Obedience, and then reading that we are to be perfect in the Beatitudes, taking these definitions to task can damage one's existence.

For instance, as a young missionary living in Brazil, I longed to be perfect, to live at such a level that the blessings of heaven would be opened to me and I would become as the voice of Paul to the world. In my attempt, I felt I should flog myself, as some religions have come to practice, and deny myself certain comforts, expecting greater rewards for proof of my Obedience.

I remember thinking I should sleep without a mattress in favor of resting on wooden slats in order to deny myself the comforts of a bed and make even my sleeplessness torturous. I smiled as my horrified mission companion watched me lie down each night on planks of wood with my mattress in the hallway, confused as to what this meant. Almost mischievously I would state, "This is my way of proving I can suffer through hard things in order to receive more blessings."

What was I thinking? It was ridiculous, but I did it nonetheless.

I would fast on a weekly basis, for days at a time, not eating or drinking anything. None of it was required by the rule book or in scripture, yet I felt it was a sacrifice that would yield blessings.

Imagine being in the Brazilian sun for 12 to 15 hours per day, walking the streets, trying to keep up energy and enthusiasm on no food, water, or sleep! It was insane!

Yet how often do we do this to ourselves by manufacturing our own version of personal suffering in an attempt to either prove something to ourselves, to others, or just simply to injure our progress? Whether it be the friend on social media who annoys you, the family member who no longer uplifts and only berates you, or the job you know you hate and could do better by walking away from but continue to slog through it instead.

This is your own personal discipline myth that you are determined to live by, and it's only hurting you!

I finally came to my senses as a missionary regarding this practice of self-torture when I became a trainer of new missionaries arriving from the United States, only to be horrified at what I was teaching them. One young man finally stood up to my preaching this concept. After a day of grueling work we had suffered through once more while soaking wet in the rain, he cried that he was ready to return home.

I had told every new missionary that they didn't need to fast for days like me, nor did they need to rid themselves of their mattresses, but that they needed to keep up with my pace, which meant we ran at all times and were never late to get home, regardless of the weather.

Running ahead of him on his third day of his mission, our trench coats were soaked in the torrential downpour, as we leaped over muddy holes in the road in our suits and dress shoes, having just left a powerful discussion in the home of an interested learner, only to realize we were late and would be breaking mission rules if we arrived home after hours.

Sprinting, freezing, sneezing, coughing, and wheezing, we ran for miles as we had missed the final bus back to our little rental. I shouted for him to keep up and stop speaking in English in order to perfect the language.

I was tyrannical. I was superhuman. Somehow I was keeping up this pace and practice in order to receive the rich blessings I thought were in store.

Finally, I turned around, only to see this young man had stopped running and I was now alone, which you aren't allowed to be on a mission. Furious that he had stopped running, I sprinted back toward him, rain beating us down, our umbrellas inside out from the wind, to find him standing over a puddle that I had just bounded over like a horse in a derby.

"What's wrong?" I shouted in the darkness and thunder. "Why did you stop?"

He was silent. Head down, mud all over his pants and shoes, water dripping from his tear-stained cheeks, he said, "I want to go home. This isn't what I signed up for."

I doubled down.

"Well, this is what a mission is. We must be faithful, we must be vigilant, we must sacrifice. If we want to bless these people, we need to be obedient in all things. Let's go!" I ordered.

He remained fixed. He said, "Hey man, you do what you have to do, but this isn't what it's about. You don't have to kill yourself, and me, in order to help everyone else. I'm done with this. I'm going to find a pay phone so I can call my parents and go home."

Admittedly, this wasn't one of those "aha" moments for me, as I was so fixed in my beliefs and ways of doing this service that I figured the process I had devised was the best way for everyone. After all, no one was getting the numbers of contacts and invitations that we were.

However, I could tell he was serious, and I didn't want him to leave, nor did I want to ruin his mission. As his trainer, I was supposed to be training him how to be an effective missionary, and I took it upon myself to train him to be the best.

I put my arm around him and said, "Let's go back to the house, get dried off, have something to eat, and talk about it before you call them."

We walked for an hour as slowly as he wanted to before finally making it to our place.

This young missionary taught me that evening as we spoke through the night that we needed to compromise, and we had to figure out a way to work together, or he would need to leave and I would need a new companion.

He said, "No more running. No more leaving a great discussion with wonderful people early just to beat the clock." He explained that there was Obedience and Discipleship, and then there was the spirit of the law.

His wise words have always stuck with me. He was right. Even though I continued my martyrdom with no mattress and fasting beyond what was necessary, we found a happy medium, he stayed on his mission, and I kept a companion who was willing to put up with my extremism.

As you consider your ways of disciplining yourself, reflect on whether you have created a monster of your own ideas about what you must suffer in order to gain blessings. My hope is that you have figured this out already and at the same time that you will take a good hard look at what you feel you must endure in order to win the battle.

You are worth more than you value yourself.

*You are worth more than you value yourself.*

Discipline is effective only when it furthers your ability to become a disciple, not merely to hurt yourself for the sake of suffering.

In learning the difference between discipline as a punishment and discipline as an art form, I have seen the power of enjoying the concept of Discipleship.

The Promise to God of Discipleship is a dedication to learning the craft of becoming as godlike as possible, rather than attempting to master the discipline. It's in the practice, not the perfection.

Consider your Discipleship. In what ways are you consistently improving your craft as a disciple of God?

It may be reading the best books, listening to uplifting music, meditating and praying aloud as you walk around the lake. In terms of associating with others, how patient and loving are you when things don't go as planned? How forgiving of yourself can you be when learning of your failings upon asking a spouse how you can improve and the truth is revealed?

These are the disciplines of becoming a disciple of God. This is your Promise to The One, meaning both to you and to God.

Obedience and Discipleship go hand in hand. Obedience is the action; Discipleship is the practice. Obedience can be moment to moment; Discipleship is consistent.

You can be obedient and yet fail in your overall Discipleship, but you can't be a disciple if you aren't obedient.

What is your Discipleship and Promise to God?

———————

This chapter could easily have been called "Intention," or "Humility," or "Truth Serum," but it all comes back to God and our Promises to Him.

As I have faced the demons that are my responses to disappointment following Service rendered with faith and charity in mind, it is clear that Intention is the grittiest concept of The Promise. Equally, Humility is the ultimate outcome of keeping The

Promise. And Gratitude is the foundation of The Promise to God, to The One, to Self.

When I look at why I do what I choose to do in my work and in my home, and how often it doesn't turn out, and how often I am angry at God because of it, I realize how incongruent I am with the message of The Promise. I figure if I spend so much time devoted to helping, serving, and delivering on my word, that things ought naturally to turn out much more often than they do.

That's just not the case.

There is no magic pill that makes this reality any less bitter to swallow, but The Promise to God is based upon Intention, Humility, and Gratitude. That's the whole shebang.

Pride is the enemy of Promise. Getting credit, recognition, justification, validation—these are all enemies of The Promise to God.

## *Pride is the enemy of Promise.*

To find it in yourself to say, "I am doing this (charity, service, extra hours at work, staying up all night to finish a project for the kids, etc.) as my Promise to God to live at my highest self, no matter the credit, no matter who knows what I did" is the most important principle to comprehend from this entire book and in your entire life.

This isn't to say to simply put on a happy face and roll over while playing dead. Don't become a wimp! This is the opposite of wimpiness. This is for the bravest, the most courageous among us.

These are the people we see doing incredible things with the intention of giving all glory to God and meaning it.

Coming to our Promise to God is a matter of submitting to God's will for us. If we can do as such and follow His path and recommendations and courageously brave forward, accepting His will for our lives, submitting to His way for us, this is the ultimate freedom in The Promise, where the true blessings are both to Self and to others.

I have only done this a few times, and it is what has made up the most significant memories and moments of my life.

Submitting to God's will to ask my future wife to marry me, despite my not having a job or work prospects—it was God's will, and it worked. Deciding to move forward in having children come into our lives, even as we couldn't make sense of how to afford making it work. Changing career paths midstream in order to save my voice, body, and go through literal hell in the process...and here we find ourselves!

God's will is greater than our understanding, and yet we must step into that stream and be willing to succumb to The Promise to God.

To be grateful while we go merrily, merrily, merrily, merrily, gently down the stream.

Sitting on your porch, overlooking the setting we painted earlier, how can you keep The Promise to God and share your gifts, and do so willingly, without pride, and without concern as to whether the actual outcome matches the anticipated one?

I know by writing this very book, as terrified as I feel in doing so, I have stepped into the stream and God sends the words through me to share with you. For He whispered to me, "Commit to sit long enough, and just write whatever you can think of, and I'll send it to you. But Promise you'll stay there."

This book is The Promise to God. My life is The Promise to God. My Family is The Promise to God. My career and the confusing and beautiful paths it has taken are The Promise to God.

What are your Promises to God?

## EXERCISE: YOUR PROMISES TO GOD

Out of the next three Service requests that come your way or that you create, pick one that is your "Heck yes!"—meaning, one that so fires you up that you would do it for free and be thrilled about it (because if it's not a full-on "Heck yes!" you're going to be mad once things get rough in the middle of your charity and Service)—and sit down and write the reasons you are fired up about this project/opportunity.

For example:

- I believe in this charity because my wife's family has suffered from this disease for generations and this is one way I can contribute by giving back.

- I will do all in my power for this event to be a success, putting my name and connections behind it, because I believe in this cause.

- I know I will not receive credit for what I have done, and most likely neither will others who are involved. When no one worries who gets the credit, then everyone wins.

- I am so grateful they chose me to help with this Service. I add great value to this cause.

That is your Promise Anchor.

> *When no one worries who gets the credit, then everyone wins.*

As you begin this project, you will keep this statement with you for a time of need. The Promise Anchor is simply your declaration of your intention before the charity work begins. It is Gratitude, excitement, and your willingness statement to do the will of God. It's your Promise to Self.

When things get tough, out of hand, and perhaps ridiculous during your project, you must talk out loud either to God or to the universe and have a chat. Express all frustration, anger, and fear. Say it, yell it—not at anyone in the room or on the phone, but at the sky. Once you've had your say, go back and read your Promise Anchor out loud.

And remember your intention.

Return to humility and God's will for you to have taken this on.

Re-establish that feeling of Gratitude, of sitting on the porch—the setting we created before—and breathe, and laugh, and sigh, and get back to work.

When your Gratitude returns, you have recommitted to God's will; let go of ego, pride, and validation; and kept your Promise once again to God.

# CHAPTER 11

# TALENTS

*There is no greater fraud than a promise not kept.*

—PROVERB

Leonardo da Vinci seemed to be touched by the hand of God with an unfair amount of talent. He excelled in nearly every venture, from drawing to painting, sculpting to science, inventing to linguistics, his refinement was legendary—even in the way he walked down the street and perfected communication skills.

Taking nothing away from his greatness and having studied his life to a level most have not, I would also dare say that he was one of the most curious, adventurous, and failed artists in history. He finished less than 20 paintings, one of which caught on fire with a revolutionary drying method he invented. He lost years to one piece, never to be completed—a mural the size of a building. Statues and sculptures remained unfinished and eventually were torn down by mobs in anger for not being completed. He was nearly killed numerous times trying out his inventions and was never taken seriously as a military mind, which he so longed to be considered. He had no family to care for and very little responsibility in relationships, and he over-promised on his abilities so often to royalty, who paid up front for his mastery, that his unfinished work made it so that he wasn't allowed in certain countries later in life.

What does this mean? It means he was obsessed with everything and that working hard on things of talent was his hobby and passion. It also means simply that he was probably born with five talents and multiplied them through experimentation and sharing them, as was taught by Jesus in the Parable of the Talents.

There have been others similar to da Vinci throughout history in terms of level of talent, none of whom have caught up to him as a polymath, but who are still revered for their mastery and Discipleship to their craft, such as:

- Amadeus Mozart and Johann Bach

- Thomas Jefferson and Abraham Lincoln

- Fred Rogers, Walt Disney, and Jim Henson

- Steve Jobs and Bill Gates

The Parable of the Talents, found in The New Testament, Matthew 25, states that one servant was given five talents, one given two, and one given one. He with five doubled his, he with two doubled his, and the one with only one talent decided to bury it instead of making more of it. Upon his master's return, the servant who was given one talent was scolded for his lack of faith in not seeking to grow his sum.

When you consider your Talents, what would you say they might be? It doesn't mean that you excel at the Talent beyond others' abilities. It may not even mean that you could make a living or a reasonable hobby of it. Having Talent simply means you tried at a particular skill and realized you could show proof that you have some capacity for it.

For example: When people hear me play the piano, they say, "Wow, what a Talent!" To which I say inside, "They have no idea. I can play only three songs...but I play them very well!"

Whether you're a master pianist or a hack like me matters not. What matters is the fact that you worked at it and then you share that Talent for the benefit of others.

Da Vinci spent his every waking moment mastering a few Talents, while dabbling in and proving he had decent capacity for many. He is considered the greatest painter of all time due to the bizarre nature by which he mastered his painting Talent. How did he paint the *Mona Lisa* smile as he did? Did you know he carried that painting around, town to town, country to country, under a cloth, unfinished, rarely to be seen, for decades while he worked at it? He rarely slept, instead tinkered through the night and then wandered the streets like a crazy man under the moon, eventually banned from cemeteries and funeral homes due to his pension for gathering cadavers to dissect and learn the muscles of the body. He was obsessed with every little piece of learning that added to his capability to understand how to paint a perfect smile. It is inspiring...and equally kind of weird.

To what level are you this way with your Talents?

The people we see who beam with the Talent glow are obsessed with their craft. They put in hours upon hours honing it, to the extent that Malcolm Gladwell termed it "The 10,000 Hour Rule," when in essence that simply gets you to Level 1. Ten thousand hours isn't considered mastery; it's your welcome to the front porch and official right to now ring the doorbell, only to enter a whole new world to explore at deeper levels you didn't realize existed.

In previous chapters, the discovery process of our Promise was laid out in a simple rhyme that is life-changing to those who can't seem to place their Talents:

IDENTIFY • CLARIFY • MAGNIFY

The process of IDENTIFYING was spelled out then, but here's another example of how this naturally works.

Eddie was terrible at everything he tried. All he wanted was to be an athlete—and specifically, an Olympic athlete. Breaking bones as he ran, jumped, bounced, and flipped, glasses flying off his face, Eddie developed the Signature Move of acquiring bruises and scrapes, and his father continued to discount Eddie's efforts.

Until one day, Eddie realized that he was going for the wrong Olympic sports. The summer events just had too much competition, so he turned his sights toward the Winter Olympics, joining the ski team and becoming decent enough to hang with the big boys.

Unfortunately, not only was he the worst on the team, but his personality and class in a caste system made him undesirable for any team, especially one representing his country. Being proper in England is more important than Talent in some respects, and Eddie was not invited to represent his country in any capacity.

Ready to give up, he noticed one event he had yet to consider: the long-distance ski jump. No one in his country represented this sport. All it took was guts enough to go off the jump and to actually land after flying through the air like a bird. The sport is considered the most frightening and insane of all jumping events.

The movie about Michael "Eddie" Edwards's life is hilarious and heartwarming, as "Eddie the Eagle" became not only England's first ski jumper to compete in the Olympics since 1928, but also accidentally ended up representing the entire country with pride once the media discovered his gift for being in front of a TV audience, morphing into one of the first reality TV stars.

Eddie realized that ski jumping wasn't his only Talent; he also had the Talents of resilience, likeability, and relatability. He became the Every Man and feel-good story of The Olympics. Despite placing last, he is the one most remembered due to his other Talents, which won everyone's hearts.

As you consider your Talents, most of the time you will say, "Well, what are my talents? I'm not good at this or that, nor am I anything like my siblings and friends who can do all of this cool stuff..."

Sadly, that's how we think. We naturally think in terms of what we aren't good at in order to name our Talent! It would be like getting asked, "What's your favorite food?" and you answer with, "Well, I don't particularly like Italian, American, Asian, Thai, and especially not Indian...but yeah, I don't know...what do I like?"

The Promise to The One is embracing your unique gifts and Talents. I have made a living out of teaching this very simple principle while sharing my Talents that most people would never show anyone else. In reality, my Talents are a collection of all the skills people do away with after elementary school in favor of growing up and being seen as respectable. And I'm fine with that, as I have found my Talents serve a purpose, when shared properly, to give permission to others to share their Talents in return.

The truth is, if you've seen what my face can do by way of movements and so forth, a majority of people can do something similar with their face. They just don't show anyone. They haven't created a routine out of it to get laughs. I just took it to a new level when it got laughs for me in grade school, so I worked on finding other things my face could do.

Who spends eight years figuring out how to wiggle their nose? Only me. But that was my level of determination to figure it out. Once the dentist told me I had control over my facial muscles, I took that to heart! I studied muscle charts, watched *Bewitched* over and over, stared in the mirror and focused for hours upon end. At the time did this appear to have any merit, this Talent I was so obsessed to discover? No! My parents were constantly begging me, "Son, please stop doing that with your face!" especially when we took family photos. I was capable of ruining every one!

But after eight years of working on moving my nose, one day as I sat on a bus looking out the window, moving my face around and focusing my efforts and knowledge and all the power I could muster on this one dream, my nose suddenly moved! I yelped and showed my friend, Denny Crockett, and he yelped, and we started laughing, and I was screaming with delight to realize I had finally figured it out!

I have since used that nose wiggle to spread joy and laughter all over the world. Yes, it creeps some people out, but in a funny kind of way. How grateful I am that I spent so much time developing that one very unique movement, a Talent which few on earth have figured out. Even if it is only a 15-second moment in my speech and show, it is easily one of the most impressive things I've ever mastered.

But mine are just a collection of random Talents that I've made fit together into a performance that is entertaining and enjoyable. I haven't mastered many things in life, but what I have created in terms of bits and routines of comedy for a show and presentation makes people say, "Wow, he has so many Talents!" And I have to laugh, because I know I have just enough Talent in each area to make you believe I have many Talents, whereas I'm teaching through show and tell that you, my friend, have your Talents, too!

It's the same with my musical Talents—I'm essentially a karaoke singer who makes a living at it. I can do voices well enough to fool you, just like every kid who's ever lived could impersonate the teacher they didn't like or the friend with the weird voice. I just continued to develop it and eventually made a living at it. But I'm not good enough to be on the radio impersonating voices...I know my limits! I can create the illusion of it all to entertain an audience into thinking, "Wow, he is so gifted! What a Talent!" My greatest Talent may be making others think I have so many Talents! But my Promise has always been to work on enough entertaining and inspiring routines, tricks, voices, songs, and dances to deliver an amazing experience to those watching for their enjoyment.

## TALENT CULTIVATION IS VERY SIMPLE; IT'S JUST A MATTER OF WHAT YOU'RE WILLING TO WORK ON.

The Promise comes into the world of Talents once you've embraced that which you have discovered and begin to share it.

This is true with every bake sale I've ever been to, where people say, "Wow, you're such a great baker!" In reality, whether the kid is or isn't doesn't matter. What matters is that they baked and shared their talents, even when everyone else on earth could do the same.

It is in the practice, commitment, and eventual mastery that you all of a sudden have a Talent for something. With enough experimenting and gumption, it can become an actual skill. That's when you are onto something and people will pay you for it.

Question is: What are your Talents? And how are you sharing them?

The truth is, we are blessed with particular Talents that must be discovered. And if we aren't exploring the options, we will never know.

I'll never forget putting our daughter in dance. She was worried everyone was going to laugh at her, as all the other girls had been dancing for years, and now here she was, trying to figure out how to move like the "pros" in third grade.

Luckily, she received the Talent of imitation on top of a natural gift for dancing, and so when she watched the instructor she simply imitated the movements and then added her natural flair, mixed with her perfectly long muscles, form, and grace, and the instructor felt she'd found a dancing savant.

Our daughter is one of the most beautiful dancers we've ever seen, and she stands out among her friends in performances. And yet even with natural Talent, if she doesn't practice as hard as those with a lesser Talent level, she won't receive the same type of praise, as natural Talent gets one only so far.

It is reminiscent of all our children entering kindergarten. My wife and I had spent a great deal of time and effort reading to the kids during the infant years and then placed them in a progressive preschool to give them an advantage once they started elementary school. At the first parent-teacher meeting, the teacher would say she was astounded at their capacity to read, communicate, and comprehend a book at such a young age.

Each child excelled throughout kindergarten, first, second, and third grade...and suddenly something happened. By 4th grade, everyone else had caught up. What happened? I'm embarrassed to admit this, but we as parents felt they were so far ahead that we didn't push them to continue to improve; we just let them do what the class was doing, and as a family we settled into normal patterns.

By the time we realized what had happened and had established Habits, reading was no longer the norm in our home, math and other skills were casually touched upon, and everyone in the grade passed our kids up as we scrambled to figure out what had happened.

When we lay off of our pursuit of Talents and cultivating our skill sets, that is when our human tendency to rest on our laurels sets in and everyone passes us by. But when we are committed to growing, learning, and achieving, that is when we make of our natural gifts a Talent that is worthy of praise and can take us far.

And so we return to the question:

# WHAT ARE YOUR TALENTS?

Your Promise in terms of Talents is to discover and nurture them to become of Service to yourself and eventually to the world.

What happens when we don't discover our Talents?

Nothing actually, and we live a life of quiet unfulfillment and disappointment for the search that never allows us to live our true meaning and share all we could have.

What happens when we discover our Talents and don't use them to full capacity?

We become something of a superhero in hiding, only revealing our gifts in moments of absolute need and without warning, completely freaking out anyone who happens to witness the miracle that is you.

For example, I was a performer at a networking event, and at the end of the night, after I received a standing ovation and people rushed up to get my card, I felt quite elated.

We eventually made our way to a sports bar in the hotel, where karaoke night was underway. Awful singer after brutal performer melted our ears with their inept belting, people looking to me for my Simon Cowell comedic response to ease our pain, hoping to encourage some to never touch a microphone again.

As the night wore on, our table buddy took his turn as we heckled and barked at how no one could sing the Journey song he had chosen.

As the chords progressed to the song's intro, as if without warning, we went from cynical to stunned as he completely slayed one of the hardest songs in the world to sing: "Don't Stop Believing." From the first line to the first chorus, we sat with our mouths open and eyes wide while he deftly created this moment unlike any I've experienced in a live setting.

If you've watched TV shows where it appears the person onstage is going to be incapable of what they've set out to do and suddenly the entire audience is in shock, that was this moment in real life.

By the end of the chorus, we were screaming and shrieking, raising phone lights and recording his performance. Women were swooning, men were high-fiving, bartenders were offering free drinks. It was as if we had just discovered Freddie Mercury and Elvis and The Beatles all at the same time, but this guy wore a business shirt and a lanyard.

As the song came to an end, we cheered for minutes. No one else wanted to get up and sing—not because they were intimidated, but because we begged him to sing some more.

He did a few more songs and continued to crush each one, as good as any singer can make a song sound. Upon him finishing, karaoke night was over, and everyone gathered around as he wiped the sweat from his brow while we badgered him with questions:

"How did you do that?"

"Why aren't you a professional singer?"

"What do you do for a living again?"

He revealed that he'd had a recording contract as a kid, but the business aspect didn't suit him. He decided to get a traditional job, pretty soon began raising a family, and he is now a salesman for a real estate insurance company.

He insisted he had made the right choice in life, and even though all of us were cheering him on to leave his job and go be on *America's Got Talent*, he said, "Guys, it's something fun I like to show now and then, but it's just one of many things I like to do."

And that was it.

We had witnessed a miracle and would be able to tell the story only from there.

Like an "Incredible" in the night, he went from SuperSuit to business suit and went back to his normal life.

If you've experienced something like this, the revelation of a Talent in a friend, colleague, child, or partner that you didn't realize was there, you know how special this moment was...and equally how sad it is when someone does something for a living other than that which we feel is their great Talent.

I understood where he was coming from, yet I also wondered what could have been for him, as he is still, in my opinion, the best singer I've heard live. And remember, I've performed with some of the top singers of all time.

This begs the question: What are the Talents you are hiding? Because they're in there.

Gay Hendricks, in his book *The Big Leap*, talks about living in one's Zone of Genius. Are you living in that space or below it?

At a wedding recently, my wife and I noticed no one was dancing. It was not the fun party atmosphere you would have thought it should be with the couple's personality. As we greeted the groom, he saw that my brother, who may be the most entertaining person alive just by nature, was there and said, "Jared, can you please liven up this party? I forgot my iPhone to have music playing, but if you could plug it in over there, there's a microphone too."

Jared nonchalantly walked over, plugged in his favorite "Wedding Playlist," grabbed the mic, and brought the house down, turning the most sedated service into a dance party celebration that felt like New Year's Eve at Times Square. People ran up to him afterward, his tie wrapped around his head, sweat dripping from his opened shirt—he looked like a rock star from *Almost Famous*—and took selfies with him. Girls gave him their numbers. Other couples told him it was the best wedding they'd ever attended and begged him to bring the same energy to theirs.

When asked why he isn't a full-time DJ, Jared just shrugged and said, "I have a job I like and the life I want, and I just do this when my friends need it." People were stunned to see how he could make something of nothing, as it is a Talent he'd cultivated through years of DJing at weddings and events. He has a natural knack for being the life of the party. We've considered getting him business cards that say, "Professional Ice Breaker for Hire," because he's just that.

I'm proud of my brother and his Talents and equally know he's chosen a certain lifestyle that doesn't pertain to running a business for himself as a DJ. It is great to know your direction and be happy with it, but it's a true Talent he has that more people ought to enjoy.

## WHAT ARE YOUR TALENTS, AND HOW ARE YOU SHARING THEM?

A speaker friend of mine asked me for some advice as we were discussing making her speech even better, more entertaining and engaging. I asked if she had any more Talents on top of her amazing characters created for poems and stories. She was already one of the most talented speakers I'd ever seen.

She said she had been hiding one Talent since her youth. In fact, she had never shown her husband or son, who was now a full-grown teenager, that she was trained as a classical pianist and wrote and sang her own songs so many years ago.

I asked if she'd send me some of what she was capable of, as I could determine whether it was worthy of the stage or not. As she began playing the piano, I wept openly. How could she have hidden this from those she loved the most? She said that upon getting married, she'd received advice to be a homemaker, wife, and mother, and to showcase the talents of her husband and children above her own.

Her piano was hidden in a storage room in her home where no one ever went, and if her family ever wasn't around, she would occasionally go in, dust off the carpet roll hiding her treasure, and play the piano softly to herself.

Can there be a sadder story than this?

When we hide our Talents, we are cheating the world of that which only we can bring.

As she revealed this Talent to her family, they embraced it so fully, so gratefully, that they bought her an electric keyboard that she could take to her speaking events and amplify the gift that so rightfully needed to be known.

> *When we hide our Talents, we are cheating the world of that which only we can bring.*

Of course, not all Talents involve music and singing. They can be anything from making a nice meal for the neighbors, to starting a business, or even to cheering on others' talents.

When my Talents as a performer were being discovered, my mentor, Chris Poulos (whom I've mentioned earlier in the book), stated profoundly, "You have more Talent in your little finger than I have in my entire body! But that doesn't mean I can't help you get in front of audiences. That doesn't mean I can't cheer you on. That's my Talent. That's the best I can offer. What can I do to help you share your Talents with others?" And he worked diligently and faithfully to help me further my career by utilizing his unique Talents as well.

Chris's greatest Talents are that of being a Connector and Cheerleader.

You may be thinking to yourself of the times you have worked so hard to reach a goal or dream, felt you had a Talent, only to realize there was an end to the road as others came along who were naturally more gifted and you decided to put the Talent to rest. This type of thing happens often to all of us. But it's what we do with the lessons learned in obtaining that Talent that matters.

Case in point: As a young high school athlete, I desired more than anything to be considered a great basketball player. I had worked hard to be good enough to make the team, but even still, I sat at the end of the freshman bench my 9th-grade year.

One day I bravely approached the coach, who was not fond of me due to my jokester personality, while he was a serious math and Japanese teacher. I asked him why he didn't play me more, offering that I was good enough and would soon be a great player.

He looked me squarely in the eyes and said, "Jason, you're not good at basketball, and you never will be good enough." And he excused me from his presence.

As a young man, I could have believed him and thrown in the towel, but this lit a fire under me that I can't even imagine this coach foresaw, as he was just speaking the truth from his perspective.

I wrote what he'd said on a white piece of paper and taped it to my bedroom mirror. I looked at it every morning and throughout the day. Next to it was my plan to prove him wrong and a set of Goals that became my Promise to myself that summer.

Waking at sunrise each summer morning, I chopped away at my Promise to myself to become the best basketball player at my school by the next season. I made 50,000 baskets that summer, ran six miles per day dribbling the ball, purchased special shoes called "strength shoes" that helped me gain almost half a foot of vertical leap, and it also helped that I grew a few inches.

I went around my neighborhood, then around my city, and then in search of the best players in the Salt Lake Valley, with the hopes of playing against anyone and everyone in order to improve. Never did a day go by that I didn't get the tar kicked out of me by better, older players, All-State athletes on their way to playing college and eventually even the pros.

Upon trying out the next season for basketball, a new coach had been hired, and the former coach, who didn't believe in me, was now the assistant, in charge of telling the new coach who was good and who wasn't. During try-outs, the new guy, Coach Greg Ezell, asked his assistant about me, as he was impressed with the way I was hustling, diving after loose balls, and not missing a shot from anywhere on the court.

Coach Ezell later told me that his assistant prepped him that I was never going to make the team. But the new coach saw something in me that he liked, and I became a starter on the varsity team, jumping completely over the junior varsity squad.

As one of the top three-point shooters in the state of Utah before shooting threes was considered a game-changing aspect, I was a mix of Pete Maravich, Steph Curry, and Dennis Rodman. You can imagine how I felt when a newspaper was handed to me at school saying I had been named to the All-State Team.

With a dream of reaching the NBA, my real Goal and Promise had been to become a great high school player, and that came to pass. There were guys on my team who were taller, better athletes, smarter, could jump higher, and naturally were more gifted.

Had they worked even 1 percent as hard as I had they would have made All-State or even All-American.

Thankfully, I had a coach like Greg Ezell who saw something in my Rudy-like determination, and despite my lack of natural Talent, he believed in and rewarded me for doing hard work to develop any Talent at all in a sport most would never think I could excel in. I became one of his most trusted players as we went on to transform the basketball program at our little private school.

I learned a valuable lesson about the gift of Talent and the hard work to create Talent—all it takes is a Promise, a commitment so strong that nothing will get in your way. I developed a Talent for basketball, a sport for which I had no natural gift, and became one of the best players around. Yet those with natural Talent were simply outworked.

So, whereas many people believe one must have Talent to succeed, I believe you must have a combination of both Talent and hard work to find true success...as well as a coach who gives you a shot.

As you're thinking about your story, the work you've put into your unique Talents and gifts, the intention is these stories will inspire you to reach for greater heights and to explore every avenue to finding all of the Talents you very well may have.

## EXERCISE: TALENTS

Consider the activities you like to do. For example, it could be writing, drawing, thinking, and creating. Now, begin writing something...anything...and become a student of the writers you love to read until you discover the Signature Moves that are yours as a writer. If you like to draw or paint, go buy a sketchpad or invest in a canvas and paints. Look up on YouTube the techniques of the craft. Study the history of artists, and explore why you feel you are one.

And then draw or paint. You must put it into practice to discover if you have Talent for it. As you work at it, you may realize you are not naturally gifted at this. If that is enough to stop you, then what is next? However, if you truly LOVE to draw or paint, then what is your motivation to keep going and improving?

Perhaps you long to do a portrait of a loved one or a landscape calls to you. Work at it; consider it your masterpiece. A word of advice is that you may not want to show anyone your work in progress until you feel it's ready to be unveiled. And regardless of what the critic says, whether good or bad, is that the end of your efforts and progression? In discovering these talents, you can now move to new levels and continue creating the Talent.

Maybe your Talent is thinking and creating...so what is it that you're creating? Is it a movie, an anime animation, perhaps an invention to improve the way a door opens or that holds your phone while you watch it on a flight? The point is, what are you doing between your thinking of the creation and actually making the Talent to create?

This exercise is simple; it's an exercise in Action.

Talents are discovered only when we pick up the pencil, dab the paintbrush, stroke the keys of the keyboard to begin writing that book or put into motion the invention you've been thinking about for way too long.

The Promise of The Talents is to use them once discovered, not only to bless your own life, but also to bless the lives of those around you. Imagine if da Vinci had never painted because he didn't bother trying, or Abraham Lincoln never gave a speech because he was too shy, or Helen Keller never tried to write because she was deaf and blind. Instead, these greats made a Promise to themselves that nothing would deter them from discovering and embracing their Talents and, thankfully, sharing them with all of us!

Take a good long moment to consider your Talents. This same process was suggested earlier in the IDENTIFY section, but a majority of people who read books rarely will actually do it. If you did already, then bravo! But if not, that's okay; do it now.

## Write out your Talents as follows:

1. Natural -

2. Worked At -

3. Want To -

This should take you a few short minutes.

Natural Talents are the gifts with which you are born, perhaps things like being funny, compassionate, and helpful.

Now consider what you've Worked At to make your Talents, such as becoming a good runner, a letter writer, an encourager and coach.

Finally, write out what you Want To make as your Talents moving forward that you have yet to try, mine being carpentry, mountaineering, podcasting, and learning additional languages.

What are yours?

And what Promises are you willing to make today to discover, cultivate, and share your amazing Talents with the world?

# CHAPTER 12

# CALLING

---

*Each day*
*I have to make*
*A new promise*
*To myself*
*To be braver than my past*
*To be stronger than the struggle*
*So I may find a bigger adventure*
*Regardless of the risk.*

—CHRISSIE PINNEY

As I write this, the wind is blowing and it's so cold I'm wearing a winter jacket in July. This is the wild weather found in the High Uinta Mountains of Northeastern Utah in the summer. So beautiful. I'm seated outside on the porch, surrounded by trees, brush, birds, and deer in my view, as cloud cover and a chill comforts my soul, compared to the beating sun that was just making me consider a retreat inside. This morning I walked four miles up the mountain to commune with God and nature, to find the

Gratitude that would prepare me to write this chapter that will serve you and me this day.

Last night I went to bed tired, hungry, and far too late. After writing in my journal deep into the night, I promised myself that tomorrow would be better than today, as I hadn't taken the time to wander into the mountains, nor even exercise, for want of having as much writing time as possible.

As the sun crept over my face through a shade I forgot to draw, birds sang and the wind blew. It was far too early to get started, but I got up anyway and put on my hiking shoes. Bleary-eyed, I walked down a dirt path through two green, creaky iron gates and up into the rock-fallen mountainside that is the view from my porch, now looking back over my writing space with fondness for the memories contained in cabins and places we have called home every summer of my life.

The walk up the mountain invigorated my soul, woke up my body, and changed what had been my perspective on writing the entire day before, as I fought through doubt, concern, validity, and ego. Bugs surrounded me with an attack that could have ruined the moment, but with flailing arms and a hat as a weapon, I staved off their blitz and laughed at the sight it must have been to any onlooking animals, fearing I must have lost my mind.

Rounding the mountaintop and finding a meadow amid the aspen groves, I watched the sun poke through gray clouds as the grass glittered with a welcome to my soul.

I'm glad I listened to The Calling this morning. It is that Voice that tells you what you ought to do, and when listened to, it makes all the difference.

The days The Calling is ignored, not just due to selective hearing, but to the needs of the world sending their to-do lists your way, is another day wasted despite all that gets done. It is one more heartbeat palpitation, one more hole in the soul.

When we make a Promise to listen to The Calling and then we keep The Promise to The One, meaning ourselves, those are the best of days. And we long to keep that feeling every day, not just the occasional happy reflection of the best parts of life we've lived.

As you read this, don't beat yourself up for the lost days and ignored moments that could have been. Instead, forgive yourself, for you did have a very valid excuse, and then make a Promise to listen next time. Each time you hear but don't act on the prompting, a piece of your life is taken, even when it feels like you made up for it elsewhere. Yet every time you listen and take action on The Calling, it adds another 100 times to your joy. Thankfully, the missed moments are not as impactful as the positive ones, which amplify life to an immeasurable degree.

The Calling happens not only at the beginning of the day and not even simply during your daily routine. Rather, there is a Calling that is so powerful it is beckoning your attention from a distance, encouraging you to begin running toward it.

You have felt this before, and you will feel it again, regardless of whether you are listening and running in the right direction or not. For the few who are on the path to living The Promise at its highest level of fulfillment, The Calling serves as a gravitational force that draws you upward. For those who hear and feel its pull, resistance can kill the soul, as you plug in your AirPods and ignore the inevitable, as you trudge to a job you have settled for and live a life you have created that is no longer one you recognize and wouldn't choose if you could do it over again.

## WHAT IS THE CALLING?

Why do we speak of it in hushed tones?

Because so few ever reach for it, and even fewer drop their guard and rush toward the abandonment of letting go and submitting to its will.

The Calling came to me at a very young age and has continued my entire life. When I listen, it expands; and as I submit, it rewards. When I ignore it, it contracts to such a focused point that it pierces my heart like a sniper, never letting go until I acknowledge it. Sometimes I have had to say, "I don't have time," "I don't care anymore," "I can't dream so big." But when I heed its invitation, make a Promise to go for it, even when I am failing it reminds me that I am succeeding.

The first book I wrote was a small pocket-sized book and not a big hit.

The second book was the first book enlarged and attempted again. Sadly, it found no audience and never manifested its purpose, even to the few who gave it a chance.

And yet I kept writing.

*The Promise to The One* is the fulfillment of this Calling right this moment. Had I believed all that was in me was the first book and then the second, both of which would be deemed failures in the eyes of the world, then I never would have pushed through to act on The Calling that has encouraged me to write this book.

I understand fully that the person reading this who has seen me on a stage will be surprised to read the way I write due to the performance they witnessed in person. The humor does not come through in writing the same way it does on the stage. But the underlying truth is the writing and this voice you are reading are the subconscious inner monologue that makes the laughs possible. Without this part, there are no laughs, because the laughter stems from a philosophy of manifesting The Calling.

And here you are.

The Calling is big-time—bigger than you, bigger than anything you've ever created. It's serious, deep, poignant, and often needs to be cradled like a baby while you sell it with a mustache and fireworks. But this is the real deal, the real space. I can write it only because I follow it and know it like my best friend and most enticing passion.

## WHAT IS THE CALLING FOR YOU?

Have you discovered it, listened to it, and followed it?

Colleagues, peers, friends, family, coaches, executives, millionaires and billionaires, celebrities and homeless people, have all asked me the same question: "How do I know my Calling?"

The answer is in the exercise that follows this next story, because The Calling isn't just one layer; it is as solid as the foundation of the Earth, with just as many options for drilling to the blazing core.

"You have more in you. You MUST share it. You have no choice, and I will not allow you to continue until you do."

Have you heard this voice before?

It may sound frightening, and to be frank, it is.

But that is the voice in your soul talking. Are you willing to listen?

A few months ago, as I performed my first of two sold-out shows in Orem, Utah, I looked out over the audience.

The entire first row was sound asleep.

Why would I admit this to you, when you would assume I'd talk only about all the good things that happen in life, the standing ovations and the accolades?

Because I'm the only one who knows the truth, the only one who can share this secret with you, and it's important that you realize what we all go through during life's performance.

The whole front row was asleep while I gave them my all.

Now granted, they were old. Probably the youngest person in that row was 97, and it was 8:10 P.M., so it was like three hours past their bedtime, but it is the truth.

And being that it was an older group in Utah County, the only drinking that had gone on before the show was perhaps purified water, prune juice mixed with Metamucil...on the rocks.

I had just performed a show that I had never done before—not in that format, not that style—and I even did four original songs, told many stories, and literally rocked these folks to sleep. I had been working on that show for a few months.

My ego was hit.

My kids waited backstage to be introduced as little raptors, and yet I almost called off the family bit to save them the humiliation of being my children. However, I went through with it and had a wonderful moment onstage with my favorite people.

After the first show, I went offstage following the very lukewarm standing ovation in preparation for the next audience filling the seats for show number two. I paced backstage as I said a prayer to God:

"What am I doing? Why did I do this show this way? Why did you tell me to do it that way?" I pleaded.

How much easier would it have been simply to have done what worked before, delivering to them exactly what they came to hear? Easy sell, killer performance—the standing ovation, no-questions-asked show.

The answer was simple—it came forcefully to my mind:

*This is how you will share the message from now on. Get used to it. Sharing your own voice is the challenge for you. It is foreign to your audience. You have accustomed them to hearing you do the voices of others; it's time to integrate and also share yours. You're 40 for heaven's sake. Trust me.*

It is one thing to get onstage and perform or speak—just the initial challenge is enough to drive most who would try away.

To have a shtick, a bit, routines, skits, that makes a difference. I know the singing impressions sell that I'm good as a performer and worth watching. I'm very good at them. Yet, vocal mimicry is a dying art. There are only a handful of us still living who make a living as a one-person show doing the voices of others in singing form. It is important that I keep delivering it.

And yet, introducing to an audience, who have paid to come see me sing like other people, the notion that I'm doing my own songs, stories, and creations, along with the impressions, that is out of left field.

And yet, it's time.

Have you heard this Calling before?

"Release the Kraken!"

It is The Promise in full force.

It's the Promise to make better Promises to yourself, in your heart, and not back down when the whole front row is asleep as you venture into the newest and latest performance that is your life.

## IT IS YOUR CALLING.

This is not to say that I'm done with singing impressions. I mean, it's a very unique gift, and one I will use forever. But at this point, it isn't the whole performance. It can't be; it's just an arrow in the quiver.

Yes, amazingly I did four original songs, a few I rarely had ever performed, one I never had. And yes, there are many more to come.

Is this a broken Promise to the audience? The paying customer? No, because I still delivered the main pieces they expected and yet this time gave them more than they knew was even an option.

The second show confirmed that these songs, this path, was the right route.

My friends, peers, and new attendees who had been dragged along were all raving about the spectrum of the performance. Some liked the impressions, but most talked about the stories, the RV and motorhome experiences, the inclusion of my children, and the original songs in my own voice that they had never really heard.

They asked to buy the songs!

A few years ago, I felt this Calling strongly—to learn to speak to an audience rather than simply do a monologue and a performance.

When the doctor tells you that your voice will wear out if you don't change what you're doing to it due to certain impressions damaging your vocal cords, that's when you start redefining what you do with it.

Speaking has become an unlikely gift.

Another arrow to the quiver that has allowed me to continue to share my gifts without damaging my voice.

Initially, it was out of my comfort zone. And then I saw the Mr. Rogers documentary...and wept like a baby.

I returned to the theater multiple times to watch it, alone, in awe of the courage of this man.

## MR. ROGERS IS THE PROMISE PERSONIFIED.

When I was a kid, he was my favorite. He was a lot of kids' favorite.

For years, and even still in some cases, he has been something of a punchline.

And yet, it is so wonderful to regain that excitement for his work and realize how ahead of his time he was. His work is more important now, even after his death, than ever before.

I feel a strong kinship with him. Not that I'm like him, but I hope to be someone like him for families, for youth, for those looking for another answer in their entertainment and learning.

Recently I was in Pittsburgh, Pennsylvania, where I paid homage to Mr. Rogers at the many places and artifacts celebrating his life and influence around his city: legendary collectibles from his TV set, handknit sweaters his Mother made, puppets who taught me life lessons that defined my youth, and a statue so beautifully overlooking the skyline—your neighborly neighbor always ready with a smile.

## FRED ROGERS WAS A LEGENDARY LEADER.

We must embrace The Promise and dare to become a punchline or, potentially, a hero in order to make a difference in the world at large.

Personally, the shift is happening. I step out onto the tightrope and continue to alter what it is I am known for, even when what I've done has worked so well. It is a natural progression, and it is necessary. Even when many don't like it, somehow many more actually do.

Why do I spell this all out for you?

Because I'd like to give you permission to listen to that voice inside of you that is telling you to live your Promise at the same time as I listen and heed it as well.

Perhaps it's a Promise you feel you never made. *But let's be honest—you did make that Promise a long time ago—*in another world, sent here with gifts and Talents that only you can offer.

Share your voice.

God whispers in your soul to remember what you said you'd do with your time here.

It's Time.

Be brave enough to keep The Promise for yourself, even when that might shift your audience for a bit.

*Be brave enough to keep The Promise for yourself, even when that might shift your audience for a bit.*

Keep your values, character, morality. Perhaps this reaffirms it. But find that place once again if it's been lost.

What scares you like a sleeping front row of people at a show scares me?

What do you know you should be doing but have put off for too long?

When you read these words, what calls to you, what provokes you to do something greater with your life, your work, your time?

In business, in leadership, in relationships, in family, with co-workers, for yourself.

Thank you for living it with me, because it is terrifying and exhilarating all at once.

And that's when you know you're living at the highest level of engagement and experience that is The Promise.

## EXERCISE: THE CALLING

Look at your job, career, life, health, faith, personality, and dreams as if you are looking from another person's perspective, but it's actually you looking at you.

Regardless of all you've done, every opportunity you've created, the perfect body you've sculpted, the wonderful relationships manifested, you need to now ask yourself:

Where is The River?

What has been waiting this whole time for me to pay attention and give myself to, and am I in it or next to it?

What is my purpose, my mission, my greatest dream and desire?

That is the entire, profound but simple exercise.

"That makes no sense," you scoff. Okay, try these examples on.

Throughout my life and career, there have been times when I have stopped midstream and realized I have stepped out of The River I was supposed to be in and instead found a cute little stream diversion that I thought was the right way. This happened when I went after my career as a performer at the very beginning, got my first job with the *Legends in Concert* as an impersonator, and suddenly realized it was incongruent with the overall Promise of my career.

So I went back to The River.

I quit the dream job of every impersonator, only to be told I'd be back, that no one ever leaves and makes it elsewhere. That was in 2002, and I haven't been or even looked back. Lots of wonderful people are still in that part of their River, but it wasn't where my River was meant to lead.

## WHERE'S YOUR RIVER?

As I began creating opportunities, we built a home as a family, welcomed the first baby, and then the second, and then the third (three kids in 26 months!). I was racing across the world performing 200 shows per year to great fanfare and making amazing money. Now here comes the fourth baby in 2011...and then I heard The Calling: "What's your Promise to The Family?"

Realizing I was rarely home but wasn't sure how to pay for our life without my excessive travels, standing in a diverted leg of The River that seemed to be the right place, I jumped to the side in an attempt to save my life and keep The Promise.

To be honest, it nearly killed me and totally derailed my entire career! But it saved my life, retained my family, and I kept The Promise.

And I went back to The River.

This seems to happen over and over again, both in career and in life, to me and anyone else crazy enough to listen and readjust to the meanderings of The River. The Calling brings me back to the place I need to be while still chasing the dream set before me originally.

It is terrifying to realize you've taken yourself down the wrong path, because momentum feels right, money and success play to the senses, and then you stop and look up from your focus in a current that appears perfect and realize you're missing The Calling and are actively breaking The Promise.

What's the most shocking experience is when you know you are living The Calling and realize there is still more and you have barely scratched the surface. That is both exciting and terrifying.

If you've followed my career and wondered, "What the heck is he thinking?" as I make drastic shifts and sudden changes that seem to derail my every progression, you've been an eyewitness to my obedience in listening to The Calling. More people have told me I've lost my mind through the years than I can count, yet they haven't understood this concept I am teaching you now. I wish there were a simpler answer for everyone to live The Calling—and some make it look easier than I do—but the hard truth is that making The Promise and heeding The Calling when it comes just might be the most insane yet most fulfilling and purposeful thing you'll ever do...and you'll need to do it over and over again. You will have to prove yourself over and over again.

From Singer to Comedy Entertainer to Father to Emcee to Agent to Philanthropist to Speaker to Writer and Author...some will come with me, most will not, for they cannot accept the path that is my Calling. The Promise to The One, to myself, is more important than any other promise I make, as this is my Calling from God.

With The Calling comes exponential progression, extreme doubt, and every blessing heaven can throw at you. If financial gifts don't manifest immediately, then the blessings of health and sustenance, love and deeper relationships, joy and fulfillment, honor and respect, all will flow your way faster than you can imagine it. Keep on your current path and those things may come and go like a soft-pitch derby, but embrace The Calling and it will be 100-mile-per-hour fastballs that allow you to crush home runs over the farthest fence. When you embrace the Calling and stop midstream to step into the River, blessings will rush toward you like water from a dam that has broken while you have a kayak ready for the ride.

As you read and contemplate your Calling, your Promise, do the exercise and stop to listen to The Calling. Are you in The River, or have you followed a path that is imitating flowing water but is really just an irrigation ditch that will eventually lead you to nothing but a drain pipe of unfulfillment?

The River, as The Calling, never stops. It is a lifelong mission, a purpose, a power so strong that you were meant to do and live and be that it will not stop flowing, enticing, or rushing. When you step into it, you will know it, and you will be swallowed up for a while. But you are in it! It is your greatest adventure. It is a journey, and there is no destination. It becomes you, and you live The Promise at full speed!

One more time, let's try this again...

## EXERCISE: THE CALLING

Where is The River?

What has been waiting this whole time for me to pay attention and give myself to?

Am I in it or next to it?

What is my purpose, mission, my greatest dream and desire?

Heed The Calling, step into The River, and live The Promise.

# CHAPTER 13

# LEGACY

---

*Overdeliver on promises and deadlines.*
*Show up early, deliver your product early, and deliver*
*more than you promised. Overdeliver now, and*
*in the future, you will be overpaid.*

—CLAY CLARK

You walk into your church and realize this isn't a regular Sunday meeting; rather, it is a funeral.

You lean toward the person next to you and ask who died, but everyone is trying to be quiet and respectful.

The meeting begins. Great song choice, a good friend of yours gives the opening prayer, and then the obituary is read.

This is your funeral.

You have one of the following trains of thought:

1. "Oh my goodness, I'm dead! What happened and why me?"

2. "Oh my goodness, I'm dead! I wonder what they're going to say."

To be given the gift of hearing what would be said during a funeral celebrating your life would be quite the experience. You may be pleasantly surprised, or you might feel disappointed by the way others see you and speak of your life. But what a fascinating thought to consider!

Now you are reading this book. Quite alive, looking good, all is well.

And that means you have what we would call the most precious gift of all: you're still here.

Your life is a combination of made and kept Promises, as well as the broken ones. The kept Promises make you legendary; the broken Promises prevent you from reaching an even higher level.

The gift today is that you get to write your Legacy. It is your masterpiece and finest creation. It is the life you will have lived, and you must illustrate it while you're living.

> *You have what we would call the most precious gift of all: you're still here.*

# EXERCISE: YOUR OBITUARY

Excluding the gory details of your absolute ending, of which you most likely can't predict, focus on the most significant statements and sentences that you would want written about your life. This is what would provoke the response from Marty McFly: "Woah, that's heavy."

When considering these sentiments, also imagine who will write this all-telling document, as one voice will differ from another. If it is your life partner, how will it sound compared to your oldest child, and then oldest child versus the youngest or middle? What about from a friend, a parent, or even a teacher from your youth? If you want to go really far, you could consider it a business partner or colleague, maybe someone you've served with in the community or church, or even just your neighbor; it's your call.

If you have a hard time with this exercise, then pick up your journal, jot a few ideas down, and then tear it out and throw the paper away, as you may be embarrassed if it were ever found.

This becomes the most vulnerable and telling writing of your life.

DO NOT settle for simple statements such as:

"She was a nice person and helped when needed."

Don't wimp out on this project! This is essential to writing your life's story as you see and want it to be told. Don't hold back. Don't beat yourself up! Don't dwell on failures. Go for the gold! Be big, be bold, hyperbole encouraged, heck—you're dead! What could be said?!

Write something like:

"She was the nicest person in the room to everyone she met, the ever-engaging smile, the ultimate encourager. When a neighbor fell ill, everyone knew where the meal was coming from and who would care for the children, as she held herself through tragedy as a hero among mortals."

"He worked every day as if he was creating the finest art, and yet gave 100 percent presence to his family, whom he cared for more than life itself. He had a superpower no one knew about until the time we needed to move a fridge down the steps and it slipped from our hands, only to be confidently manhandled by him alone, down the steps to the U-Haul. He never ceased to amaze us."

You may think this is ridiculous, but it is a key to living the most legendary, fullest life and creating the Legacy you see possible for yourself. The Promise extends beyond this life, and you must work on the fulfillment of it now.

So, Exercise 1 is to compose your obituary.

## EXERCISE: YOUR ADJECTIVES

Exercise 2 is a list of words you would like to be used to describe you.

Such as:

- Godly/ Christlike

- Faithful

- Confident yet Humble

- Engaging

- Optimist

- Leader

- Brilliant

- Family Man/Woman

- Genius

Take a few minutes to write yours down.

No need to show anyone; that would be embarrassing, most likely. Having written them in your journal or notes, now you have the outline that becomes your story, your words, your life to create.

Now make a Promise: Become that person.

———————

Before your deadline on earth, consider another deadline: Your Creations.

It has been said not to let the music die within you. This is profound and so often sadly the case, as life and details get in the way of us finishing what we most wanted to.

# EXERCISE: TO-DO LIST BEFORE I DIE

It may sound like a morbid way to look at it, but the wording for this exercise actually profoundly impacts the way you will get to work. Here's the exercise—

Write a list of the ten projects you want to live on after you. It could be anything from updating the scrapbooks to writing out all of your Grandma's recipes. Perhaps it's a genealogy and stories told that you record in your Voice Memos on your phone, or the album of music you've been meaning to record. More people have a book in them than any other project I've heard talked about—yet how many get it done? It may even be something as simple as calling your child or parent and asking forgiveness for something that was said. Burdens lifted all around.

You choose, but make a Promise to get the list written, and begin chopping away at it as if you're on borrowed time...because actually, we are!

Set a deadline for each project.

Tell your accountability partner that you promised to do this crazy list and they need to make sure you do it.

Now go do it!

# CHAPTER 14

# VALUE

*The promises of this world are, for the most part,
vain phantoms; and to confide in one's self,
and become something of worth and value is
the best and safest course.*

—MICHELANGELO

*Weekly I write a blog called (and I know this is a shocker)
The Promise, and thousands of people wake up to it in their
e-mail inbox on Sunday mornings, without fail, no matter
where I am in the world. Unless some major technical glitch
happens, it's my Promise always to deliver this.*

*I have been told the blog should be a book in and of itself,
which is very kind; however, I thought it appropriate to
include in this section on Value a collection of stories that have
resonated the most with readers and will add much Value to
this book. Commentary prefaces a few of the stories for refer-
ence and explanation. I hope you enjoy.*

# WHAT ARE YOU WORTH?

Recently, I have received, no lie, over 10 requests for events from local businesses asking essentially the same question:

"What is the lowest you can do your speech for our company's most important event?"

I understand everyone wants a deal. Heck, I WANT A DEAL for everything I want, and am unwilling to pay for, as well.

However, I've NEVER walked into the finest restaurant in town and said to the hostess,

"Hey, real quick, before you seat us, we know this place is like $200 per person, but we are looking to get this lavish meal for somewhere in the $12.50 range. I'm assuming you'll pull out all the stops for us since we're a pretty big deal and it may land you some opportunities in the future when we tell our people about you."

I mean, that sounds absurd.

Or better yet, how about going to the best lawyer, dentist, tailor, or doctor in town and having that conversation?

My friend, here's the real question:

*What are you WORTH?* In your own mind? In your market? At your hourly wage?

Professionally, not spiritually, we are talking numbers here, so be frank.

I just firmed up an event for my full fee with a company that originally came to me over a decade ago with a lowball offer.

I told them "no thank you" way back then. They pleaded, "It's a tight year, tough times. This is a big opportunity for you"—all of the claims, while I knew their event was at the nicest hotel, with the finest dining options, the biggest sound and lighting package, and the top speakers in the universe. But since I'm a local guy and they're a local company who is a big deal, I should desire to have their logo on my client list?

They offered me 10 percent of what my fee was back then.

Here we are, 10 years later. I've told them "no thanks" with every offer for a decade. Now my fee is 50 percent more than it was.

And I just confirmed it today.

I got the e-mail confirmation, looked in the mirror, tipped my hat to myself, and said, "Nice," and sent the contract.

Once again, I ask: What are you WORTH?

I could have folded, talked myself into every reason for doing so (but then I'd hate myself), but in the end it all comes down to one thing—

## I PROMISED myself I would retain what I feel my Value is.

And it took a decade to make it happen.

What amount of time are you willing to wait while all the rest of the world catches up?

Because heck, I know what the market will bear, I know what I am offered over and over, and I also know that the client will come away screaming that they underpaid me. I like being of such high value for the price tag in that space.

*What amount of time are you willing to wait while all the rest of the world catches up?*

Just last week as I came off the stage, having done my show for a very large local company, the client ran up raving, "WOW! We have had Jerry Seinfeld, LeAnn Rimes, Brian Regan, and all kinds of legends in the past as our entertainment. You just topped them all...and you live in South Jordan, Utah? Why?"

I replied, "I'm thrilled you were pleased, and thank you for the compliments. Truth is, those artists come with a certain expectation due to their fame, and a large price tag; plus they come in from some big city. I know my place, I know my Value, I know what will be delivered, and I'm honored you'd say I am in that category. Thank you for having me and helping me feed my family. I'm very grateful to be the affordable option to the big-name celebrity."

That's what I deliver, that's what I do, and I love being that guy.

And I know you have questioned your Value as well.

And you've folded. More than you should have. As have I.

But since you're reading this, I'm asking you to really buckle down and ask yourself, "What is your Promise to YOU?"

THAT—whatever you've decided it is—IS YOUR PROMISE!

This thing called The Promise isn't just some philosophical, ethereal, mumbo-jumbo concept...

This is game-changing, business-altering, bottom-line moving, glass-ceiling shattering, proven stuff here, my friend!

Can you hear me screaming yet????

"WHAT ARE YOU WORTH?!?!?!"

*You know how you can be in the flow, working diligently on a project in the house, and suddenly someone stops by and invades your time and space?*

*What are you supposed to do?*

*The Promise to be Kind comes to mind, yes, but you also have to keep The Promise to Value your time and what you were working on.*

*How often this type of situation has happened to me! And I've had to be very candid with the person who arrived unannounced by saying simply, "It is so wonderful to see you. I only have about five to ten minutes to chat. I have a huge project I'm working on, and this is my only time to finish it."*

*If you don't say that and establish the deadline or what you intended to do with your day, then other people can gobble that time away. This is a practice of self-worth and value, rather than doing what everyone else wants or needs all the time.*

*The Promise to The One is very much focused on protecting your boundaries, your time, your philosophies and ideals, and especially your morality and the value you feel you bring the world.*

*In the following story, I shared this decision with the world, and the response was extremely supportive, although I was blasted by some very dear friends and family who did not agree with me. It came at a politically divisive time in our country, as well as a moment when sensitivities ran so high that I needed to stand for what I felt was right for those in the audience.*

*This is The Promise not only to those in the crowd, but to me, in order to maintain what I feel is the highest of Integrity and Value whenever I take the stage.*

# LEAVING NEVERLAND: SAYING GOODBYE TO MICHAEL JACKSON

The moonwalk is what set my career in motion.

I knew that if a gawky, awkward, dweeby, girlfriend-less kid like me could figure out that incredibly beautiful, other-worldly move, it was game over.

For an entire summer I wore out my VHS tapes of *Motown 25 Special, Making of Michael Jackson's Thriller, Moon-walker,* and every MTV performance I could capture, rewinding and pausing each magical movement Michael Jackson did with his feet, legs, shoulders, neck, head, arms, hands...sometimes dancing in my basement for 12 hours a day.

My parents eventually made me put a piece of plywood down as there were scratch marks all over the parquet floor.

After an eye-opening experience as a teen where I embarrassed myself impersonating him, I made a promise I would only perform a routine of MJ that was G-rated, and thus would be the path of my career: *Family Friendly First.*

When I got my first real job as a performer, working for the Las Vegas *Legends in Concert* as a full-time impersonator, every friend from my past figured it would be as the Michael Jackson impersonator. They didn't realize you had to look just like him to work there. Thus my simple transition to dancing like and channeling Ricky Martin, who does many of the same moves as MJ.

Leaving *Legends* I put together a one-man show of music and comedy impressions. It was very successful very quickly—and, most importantly, my Promise was to keep it family friendly—always.

If you know my headlining Las Vegas casino story, then you know family first is what it's all about when it comes to my performing.

And while Michael Jackson has remained the very singular, most prominent character in my arsenal of impressions (while classics such as Jim Carrey, Led Zeppelin, Metallica, and others have been retired due to physical injury), even the very crux upon which I base my entire presentation due to his legendary moonwalk, helping others consider their own "Signature Moves" with the question, "What is your moonwalk?" then you may realize I have a situation staring me in the face as of this very moment!

I guess I'll once again quote what naturally comes to mind, since it fits perfectly:

"I'm gonna make a change, for once in my life...it's gonna feel real good, gonna make a difference, gonna make it right."

*The Promise of Becoming a Legendary Leader* isn't just something I coined and created—it's the basis of my existence.

I believe all of us have the ability to make something of ourselves with our unique gifts and can all become effective leaders as we discover our Signature Moves.

Utilizing the dancing of Michael Jackson in every performance of mine for over three decades has taught that principle masterfully, as everyone has tried the moonwalk and failed at it, which helps us realize we are all individually and uniquely gifted.

With the latest allegations and controversy, and in respect to those that have come forth now a decade since MJ's passing, having watched the new movie and documentary called *Leaving Neverland*, interviews, and backlash, it is with much sorrow, and equally determination to do what's right, that I say goodbye to presenting Michael Jackson in my performances.

Is he guilty? Is he innocent? It's not for me to judge or determine. If what has come to light is the case, then it's despicable and I choose to distance myself from it.

I know my actions onstage, as a speaker and performer, and my promise is to always do what I feel is intrinsically right, even if it means a very uphill challenge for me to replace and start over.

For the past week I have been working overtime to erase YouTube videos, hire editors to re-edit my new videos to make them appropriate as to this decision, changed my entire website—you name it. This is a problem for me on a very large scale and yet something very necessary to face head-on immediately.

For my audience, for those learning, listening, trusting me with words that evoke emotion, inspiration, laughs, and even tears, it is to inspire each individual to move up and never to suggest insensitivity or callousness.

I apologize to any I have unknowingly offended in my having performed the Michael Jackson routine for so long and for using him as an example in leadership.

His music, dance moves, and memory remains. He created quite the legacy as an artist, and it is up to us whether or not to enjoy his artistry in private and with our own need for the emotions he brings.

My promise to every audience is to bring joy, and in that promise the glove has now gone from its permanent place in my travel bag to the moving-on bin.

It's hard to say goodbye to something I have worked so hard to be good at, but it's necessary.

That is The Promise.

*There is a choice that needs to be made between setting our Value, The Promise of what our life can be, and living simply day to day with no aim and taking what comes at us. If we Promise ourselves that we will make the choice earlier in life, we will set ourselves up for greater success.*

*The following story gives perspective into how and why these choices, and our definition of our own Value, matters right now.*

# THE CHOICE BETWEEN

Two Mondays ago we welcomed the newest member to our family, a beautiful, excited, chew-everything, diarrhea-everywhere, happy Goldendoodle eight-week-old pup.

His name is Buster Silvermine Bojangles Dude Hewlett.

We love him.

As we got all set up, after a trip to the store to buy a kennel, bed, and chew toys, the time quickly passed from P.M. to A.M. as the kids were still up playing after midnight with our new little friend.

Suddenly, I heard an explosion.

No one else heard it, as they were making noise with the dog, but as the Dad I seem to hear everything.

Running outside there it was: A white car smashed into the neighbor's Ford Explorer that is always parked in front of their home.

No tire marks, no brake engaged, simply a smashed little white car into a vehicle twice its size, and it had pushed it over 10 feet forward. I bet it was going over 40 on a 25 mile-per-hour street.

A man came tumbling out of the driver's side, wincing, choking, swearing up a storm in agony.

I shouted, "Dude, are you okay?"

He ran.

Down the street, up on the sidewalk, gimp-limping away with what appeared to be a broken leg.

I ran after him, shouting, "Hey, are you okay? Let me help you!"

He turned and ran toward the neighbor's yard, attempting to leap a fence taller than him.

I continued running, "Bro! Stop. Come lay down. Let me help you!"

That's when he turned, looked me eye to eye, and began charging toward me with his hands in his hoodie...

In a split second, I thought, *Maybe he has a weapon?*

I ran toward him anyway, because he seemed to need help and was disoriented.

Grabbing him, we both went to the ground, as he continued shouting words I can't write here. In pain and anger, he moved, writhing and gagging as if to throw up.

I finally got him to calm down enough to tell me his name and I told him he'd be alright.

The neighbor called 911, my wife brought out a blanket as he lay on the cold, wet, snow having just dissipated grassy lawn.

As he whimpered and moaned, I tried to talk to him, check his leg to see if it was broken, and did all I could to comfort a stranger.

Looking at his car, it was totaled. No smoke came from it so we seemed safe next to it, and we awaited the police.

When the first officer arrived, he casually walked up, shined a flashlight down on us, and clearly stated, "Well, hello there (full name, first and last). What drug is it tonight? Meth or heroin?"

I asked, "You know him?"

The officer never acknowledged me; rather, he continued with the suspect: "You've been in jail for a year, buddy, out a week, and now this? When will you ever make the right choice?"

As I processed the situation, I decided to remain there and make sure the blanket was under his head as a pillow, while the officer made him show his hands and checked him for weapons.

Eventually, the ambulance and fire truck pulled up quietly, no sirens, bandaged up his leg, and then grilled him for 30 minutes on our curb before handcuffing him and taking him to jail.

Woah.

What a night.

I had a hard time sleeping.

What if he'd had a weapon?

What if that was my last moment on earth?

Trying all I could to help a stranger, be a Good Samaritan, and instead be the victim of a terrible crime in front of my children watching from the living room window?

Upon further reflection, I realized there's a choice between the life we live and those we could live.

I've known this forever, but it becomes clearer as life goes on and we face what could have been.

At some point, that young man decided to try a drug that affected his thinking, eventually addicted him, and he has since paid the consequences and will continue to wreak havoc on society.

I remember the first time I was offered a drug, and even though I turned it away, I'm no better than this young man in the sense that I too have fallen into my own self-destructive habits and addictions, be it staying up too late, eating too much, or being judgmental of others.

I'm no better than him in that sense, but I know I've tried to make good choices in the long run.

And I'm the guy who will always run toward someone needing help. That's a promise I never made consciously; it's just intrinsically in my DNA.

The choice between doing good with our lives and doing bad is such a fine line it's astounding.

And it's equally wonderful.

We are blessed with the free agency to act as we will, and if we contribute to society positively, most often good will come of it.

Conversely, if we break the law and make a mess of things, we will be punished, either by the law or by what we create of our relationships and the ultimate destruction of all things we hold sacred.

It all comes down to a choice between which kind of life you decide to live.

Repenting and changing is possible, yet often the grip of addiction can ruin us and those around us.

The question for you is what choice have you made in your past that has led you to any place of discontent?

If you're like me, you started biting your fingernails at age four and haven't stopped. Perhaps someone called you ugly the first day of school and you accepted that as your life-long curse, or maybe you believed you were bad at math in fifth grade and it affected you the rest of your life, even until the point your daughter asks for help with her home-work and you are now passing the belief on to her...

It still remains a choice in these moments and times. I can still fix it. I can still change. It's just a choice between what-ever promise I make to myself and those around me.

## What is your choice right now, and what kind of life do you promise to lead?

*In earlier chapters, we've discussed Talents, IDENTIFYING our gifts to use them for good, and yet we haven't touched on what happens when your body sabotages you and the Talents must be reconsidered or retired.*

*This has been one of the most difficult parts of my career, which I have rarely revealed until only recently, as so often people who enjoyed my "old show" would wonder aloud why their favorite parts were no longer included. In essence, they were saying I had broken a Promise to them in not doing their favorite routines and not performing my greatest hits.*

*Here's the answer I now give. For you I ask,* in what ways are you hurting your present while sacrificing the future? *It is The Promise to The One, yourself, that is most important, and the one way you can continue to bring great Value to this world as only you can.*

*In what ways are you hurting your present while sacrificing the future?*

## THE PROMISE OF SELF-PRESERVATION: MY LEGENDARY JIM CARREY IMPRESSION

As the physical therapist strapped weights to my forehead pulling back, and weights to the stem of my neck pulling forward, he looked at me and asked, "How long are you going to keep hurting yourself?"

It had been six months of intense fixing: chiropractors, yogis, personal trainers, physical therapists, and anything I could justify trying to keep getting onstage, save becoming addicted to crippling and numbing drugs.

It wasn't just the body falling apart, it was my voice as well.

Coming offstage with nothing left, the pain was too much. But at least the audience was entertained!

ENTs sticking cameras down my throat let me know surgery would come soon to remove damage long ago done and what I had put my voice through over 12 years of pushing the extreme limits of the human voice was destroying my God-given gift.

At 36 years old, I was given a grim diagnosis—keep doing what you're doing on stage, and you will be dead by 50.

For one moment, I'd like you to consider what is your great gift, and how you've utilized it your entire life not only to be successful in work, but also to engage friends, make people like you, and be all you've banked on for your future as well.

And now you're being told you have abused it and will lose your *Signature Moves* very soon if you don't pivot.

### The Promise of Self-Preservation is simply The Promise to The One.

At some point I had to admit that it was worth it for me to become healthy, to not have to suffer any longer, and to adjust my life.

### What in your life needs to shift NOW?

Perhaps you are burning the candle at both ends just to make ends meet.

Maybe you are doing the work of multiple people because your employer has no idea of the missing pieces.

Some may be in a relationship that long ago should have changed, ended, whether it be someone you live with or just a friend on Facebook who needs to have a conversation that it's over....

### My friend, what are you doing to keep The Promise to yourself of health, dignity, self-care, and sanity?

This is a painful conversation to have, but you may be pushing yourself to such a degree that you will not last at this pace without a major change immediately.

I'll never forget the discussion with my wife, and then my family, that I was done with a lot of things that had made me successful.

We had to sell precious parts of our life away, make adjustments that were so difficult and sad, and yet it all was necessary to continue moving forward while still allowing me to be a functioning person.

A casualty of this decision was to retire some of my Greatest Hits: Led Zeppelin, Metallica, Guns N' Roses, and many others. Once in a while, I still try them to see if they're still there—and wow, the suffering I experience is just not worth it.

Perhaps the most tragic was leaving behind the Jim Carrey working at a Subway routine, considered by many to be my best impression.

Ever since my first show over a decade earlier, I had ended with the Jim Carrey routine, throwing myself to my back, a guaranteed standing ovation at every show.

Now it was done, as it proved to be the most painful part of my act on my neck and body.

I have since recovered, have changed my career into a keynote speaking performance where only those acts that aren't hurtful remain.

## But the question is: What do you need to STOP doing to preserve yourself?

Perhaps even letting go of that good thing you do now will help you discover the BETTER career and life that lies ahead?

I know it has for me—even though many people still ask, "What happened to our favorite Jim Carrey routine?"

What's your Promise to YOU?

*Value comes in all shapes and sizes, and sometimes The Promise to The One is simply to do something great, whether anyone realizes what you've done or not.*

*The Value we place on an item at a store that was made in another country is going to be different than the Value we place on a piece of art we saw the artist create.*

*This next story may be one of my all-time favorites due to the fact that it drives this point home and leaves us dreaming bigger, shooting higher, and making Promises that bring a Value of such depth that someday someone will shout, "You made this?!"*

## "YOU MADE THIS?"

Have you ever been to an art gallery, walked around casually observing the paintings, and then stumbled upon the sight of the artist at the easel, apron and paint brush in hand, in the back of the room working on an actual piece of art?

From what was a gallery of nice overlooked trees, mountains, and landscapes, to realizing, "Oh my heavens! Someone truly painted that!"

It's almost like you've just discovered a whole new appreciation for every last little detail when you open your eyes to what someone created, but only when you realize the person who created it is in that very room.

This happened to me when my friend and fellow keynote speaker, Clint Pulver, mentioned to me that he was taking down the circus he'd built in his home.

I figured it was just some fun hobby model set he'd collected throughout the years.

I drove 30 minutes to his home, out of respect for what sounded like it was something really important to him and to show my support for his little project.

He allowed me to open the door to the room that would soon be his firstborn's bedroom, and I would be one of the last people to see Clint's circus creation thing he'd tried to tell me about.

As he watched me, I did my best impression of being impressed and delighted. In all honesty, I just thought it was cute and creative, seemed like a bunch of work, albeit a bit weird and childish. I mean, who puts a circus in a room in their house from things they've collected and invites their speaker pals to come and see it?

As I did my best to find things to ask him, I looked closely at each figurine and wondered aloud, "Man, where did you buy all of this stuff? It's very intricate."

That's when Clint realized I hadn't understood what this was.

"Jason," he said, "I didn't buy this. I MADE IT. From scratch. Every piece of cloth I bought from Hobby Lobby; every person and figurine I melted and molded and painted by hand. Every leather and wire rein on the horse and elephant I cut with wire cutters, shaping them through the night. I even made this one part out of a 7-Eleven Big Gulp cup! Nearly everything you see I made with no instruction manual, a circus honoring my grandfather's memory to a model scale."

I blinked...and blinked again.

It was starting to hit me.

"YOU MADE THIS?" I shrieked.

"YESSSS!" he laughed.

"WHAT!?!" I couldn't compute what he was saying. "YOU MADE THIS?!?"

"Why do you think I wanted you to see it before I tear it down, pack it away, and make room for the baby?" he asked.

I was now stunned. Shocked in every way. Previous to my understanding, it had meant really nothing to me as he briefly explained that I should make the trip to see it, and now I felt as if I had just wandered into the workshop of da Vinci having just completed the *Mona Lisa*.

I speak in hyperbole for a living, but for me, this was one of the greatest creations I've ever seen.

I started to cry.

I begged him to wait to tear it down so I could bring my kids to see it the next day.

I canceled meetings and pulled them from school to see this.

I watched a four-hour documentary about *The Circus* on Netflix all night.

After having spent one year creating all by himself in a room in his home, Clint produced one of the most magical artistic spectacles I've ever witnessed. It inspired my Art and Promise to myself to get to work on a few things that might make someone someday as exasperated and stunned as I was and potentially ask me,

"YOU MADE THIS?"

Yes, he made pretty much every little thing you would see in this circus, with few exceptions, and it's as magical as any Promise ever kept in honor of his grandfather and the joy of his love of the circus: *The Willie Clinton Circus!*

Truth be known, he was never going to show this to anyone; he made it just because he wanted to. One evening, a friend accidentally opened the door to the room, thinking it was the bathroom, and Clint shared what he had made.

From then on, people streamed from the home, as Clint announced the Circus would have to come down to make way for the newborn baby.

It took Clint over a week to deconstruct his year-long project, pack it up, and put it in bins and storage to be brought out again someday when the Pulver Family expands enough to need a larger abode, which will house The Willie Clinton Circus once again.

What a joy to see it in person, what an honor to see the greatness that is someone keeping a Promise to themselves to make something of such value...and to think no one was going to see it!

What are you creating that will one day make someone shout in shock and delighted surprise,

"You made this?!"

# EPILOGUE

---

*The Promise is your clarion call to Commitment, your investment in Integrity. It's your Purpose, your Proclamation, and your Legacy.*

—JASON HEWLETT

The Promise to The One is the most important place to start on the journey to living a life of Promise Making and Keeping, which will lead to greater joy and fulfillment.

This is only the beginning.

So many elements of The Promise will be coming forth to the world in books to come, such as *The Promise to The Family*, *The Promise to The Audience*, and many more.

We began with *The Promise to The One*, which is you, because so often we give our all to those we serve at work, those we live with at home, and essentially everyone else. We are naturally selfless in that way, and it is a beautiful and important way to live.

However, when we break The Promise to The One, to ourselves, there will be little we can give to others. A starving horse can't pull the cart.

Please Promise yourself that you will take a moment for you, daily, weekly, however often you need, to re-evaluate this one principle. We have just completed an entire book on one principle! Thus the importance of it.

Continually ask yourself, "What is my Promise to me?"

And then, "Am I keeping my Promise to me?"

As you do, you become a person who lives fully every chapter title listed, a person of Promise who is strong, prepared, and ready for all life throws at you.

My blessings with you, and my gratitude that you'd join us on this journey. I invite you to continue on this journey as more books come forth. Videos, podcasts, online trainings, and live events await your very much needed Signature Moves that will uplift and honor all attending, reading, and inspiring.

There is no one like you. There never will be again. You are here for a purpose right here and now.

Keep The Promise to The One.

# MEET
# JASON HEWLETT

## PERFORMANCE COACHING

One of the youngest inductees in the prestigious Speaker Hall of Fame, having delivered thousands of presentations over two decades, Jason is among the most sought after mentors, coaches and speakers worldwide. His clients call him the world's premiere coach and speaking authority for successful leaders looking to create greater influence through powerful messaging and personal branding. Now is your time to coach personally with Jason, contact us to learn more.

## KEYNOTE SPEAKING

Purpose driven engagement, proven performance results, teamwork, change, accountability and the profitability of integrity are the core messages within Jason's dynamic one-of-a-kind stage presentation. No keynote speaker in history combines the talents of Las Vegas performance, uncanny music impressions with legends of stage, comedy unparalleled, with business examples and heartfelt stories that change lives in one message. Bring Jason Hewlett's speech of The Promise to your next event for an unforgettable, life-altering, business bottom line impacting leadership talk your attendees will rave about for years to come.

Contact Jason today:
jason@jasonhewlett.com
801-674-3668
JASONHEWLETT.COM

## THE HEWLETT FAMILY

The Hewlett Family enjoys summers in the RV crossing America, creating memories, and spending time together. When not speaking on stages around the world and coaching executives in leadership and performance, Jason is coaching his boys in basketball and his daughter in skiing, as well as writing viral posts about how much he loves his wife.

They reside in Utah, where hiking, adventure, and serving the community make for a wonderful life. Jason's hobbies include writing music, mentoring aspiring and successful speakers, and spending quality time with his family attending Utah Jazz games, visiting national parks, and hosting get-togethers with extended family.

# NOTES